DETERMINED Life

A POOR MAN'S HOLLYWOOD

WRITTEN BY TEI'ASHA DE'ANNE

MW01172756

Copyright © 2024 Tei'Asha De'Anne Simms

All rights reserved

No part of this book may be translated, reproduced, or transmitted in any form or by any means without prior permission from the Author.

Cover Art: Autumn Joe Ellis

Author Photo: Tae Stubbs

Book Cover Design: Sam

Editing: Abuzar Siddique

Formatting: Abdul Moiz

Publisher: Tha Book Lady

DEDICATION

From Darnell Walker,

"Dedicated to Derrick,

I dedicated my book to a person who instrumentally help me become the man I am today. Derrick played a big part in my life. He was and is everything to me. He was my protector, my father, my uncle, my brother, and my best friend. He taught me a lot, and I learned a lot from him. I miss him dearly. God wanted him with him instead of with me. I didn't lose him completely; I gained an angel who is still protecting me. My work is not done here. I love you, and I miss you. Peace and loyalty, the Saga still continues..."

CONTENTS

INTRODUCTION

I t always has a price. Freedom has always been one of the most expensive tickets for black men and women to purchase. It also appears differently for each individual. We fight so hard for our version of freedom, but at what cost?

This is the story of Darnell Walker, a man from Detroit, Michigan, who spent years trying to free himself from his addiction to the streets. He couldn't get out of the street life. It was his Hollywood, it had a hold on him and had become all he knew. Even with multiple attempts to take his life, it still didn't keep him out of the streets. When Darnell finally did get his freedom from the streets, it cost him 25 years of his life.

25 years was the price he had to pay and even though he was freed from the streets, he had become chained to the prison system. Some would say that doesn't sound like freedom at all, but it depends on where you're standing. After being incarcerated for 25 years, his true freedom kicked in, and he came back to rebuild the same community he had helped destroy.

While others sometimes use their stories to bury themselves, he decides to use his story to plant seeds. This is just the beginning of those seeds starting to sprout. Darnell was and is determined to get his life back. So, lock in and pay attention, most importantly, don't miss the message.

Chapter 1
TAKE ME BACK

W e all know you can't tell a story without starting from the top to paint the picture. Let's go all the way back to the 1970s. Darnell Walker was born and raised in Detroit, Michigan, along with his older brother Derrick and mother Sharon. Darnell's father was not very active during those early years, and his mother made sure to shield him from a lot of the struggles of that relationship. She did everything to protect him from knowing anything about the abusive relationship she was in. Because of that, he never really knew a lot about what his mother was going through, nor did he have much of a relationship with his father. Not one that he could remember at least. She finally gathered the strength to leave and for a short while it was her and her two boys.

Darnell and Derrick would have been described to be night and day. While Derrick was the outspoken, say whatever comes to mind type of kid, Darnell was the complete opposite. He was quiet and never really talked much unless pushed to. He wasn't too sociable, nor did he like to be outside much. Trying to get Darnell to talk was like pulling teeth. He was never one of many words. He and his brother shared the average sibling war relationship all through their early years. Derrick would spend most of his time picking on Darnell until he would finally get the reaction he was pushing for. Sharon would give their family and friends the necessary disclaimer to not push him. Although he was quiet, he was not one to sit back too much before exploding and her having to hear about it. She could always tell which son someone was telling on by what they said they did.

With Darnell being the youngest, there was a lot of love and attention his mother felt she had to over compensate for. Derrick, being the first grandchild and great-grandchild, resulted in a lot of outpouring of affection for him from his dad's side of the family, leaving Darnell looking and feeling left out. On top of their father's absence, the difference in the way they were treated was noticeable, and she paid attention to it. That created a soft spot that his mother had for him. She never wanted him to feel like he was not as important or as loved as his brother. She made sure to try and give him whatever she felt he wasn't getting. Eventually, by the time Darnell rolled into his early teenage years, he started to use that as his advantage to get out of doing things his mother wanted him to do or doing the things he was not allowed to do. He would use it to get out of housework, be disciplined, and even go places he didn't want to go. At that point, being "the baby" was his trump card.

A little while later, Sharon met a man who stepped in and became the father figure in her boys' lives. He would get them involved in different types of programs to keep them off the streets. He started teaching them karate and even went on to get them started in boxing. Darnell took really well to boxing, much more than karate. Darnell describes their relationship like any other. There were good times and bad. He taught Darnell some things that he remembered and carried to this day. However, one day, they wiped almost everything away, and their relationship was never the same. At that time, Darnell was in junior high, attending Cadillac Junior High for 6th, 7th & 8th grade. However, he had been suspended so frequently that he had only completed half of his eighth-grade school year before being transferred to Redmen Junior High. He had been having a lot of trouble with his behavior and academics in school. Darnell never showed much interest in what was being taught. Other than math, because of his love for numbers, academically, Darnell had a struggle in learning. One of his biggest struggles had been reading. He would never want to read out loud or didn't really understand the material. On top of his academic struggles, he was constantly being kicked out. Following one of his many suspensions, he returned to school and was suspended again the same day. His stepdad was waiting for him at home. Now, Darnell used to get whoopings, but that day was different; he was left with welts and bruises on his legs. The bruises were so severe Darnell's mother took him to the hospital to get checked out. During that time, Darnell was silent, not answering many questions, just making it clear that the bruises were not from the hands of his mother and left it there. He said nothing else for hours. The first thing he said when he got home was directed to his stepfather. He said, *"You ever touch me again, I'll kill you."* He meant it. A flick switched for him that day; not only was their relationship over, but he also intended that message to be sent to anyone who would consider touching him in the future. From that day forward, Darnell went cold, and his relationship with school never got better.

As the years went on, Darnell became a lot more sociable and started to hang out in the neighborhood, making friends. One of those friends that stuck was Aaron, also known as "Mann." Mann was also said to be a quiet one of not too many words himself. He and Darnell would hang around each other so much that they later found out they were actually blood brothers, and you probably wouldn't have seen one without the other. Derrick had a close friend that stuck around as well. His name was Curt. The neighborhood they were hanging out in gave them a very distinctive name. A name not many would understand. The streets they were handing out on were Grand River and Robson. There was a vacant, rat infested house they would always hang out in front of. One day, someone killed a rat and nailed it to the house. Ever since then, they were known as "River Rats". That is how everyone knew them.

Darnell's routine suspensions had let up, and his academic performance had gotten better by the time high school rolled around. He had started his 9th grade at Cody High School. Mann ended up moving in with Darnell, and they attended Cody together. Cody wasn't in their old neighborhood, and it definitely made a difference for Darnell. He had taken a welding class that he loved, had not gotten suspended, and his grades had progressed.

By the 10th grade, he begged his mother to transfer him to Cooley High School to get back to his old neighborhood, and against her better judgment, she allowed him to go. Mann's mother still lived in the old neighborhood so Mann moved back with his mom and Darnell went with him. Although he kept his grades intact his time at Cooley High didn't last very long. Darnell and Mann had gotten caught up in a riot when a group of guys surrounded them in the lunchroom. As one of them began to approach Mann from the side, Darnell threw a punch and then he and Mann began throwing any chair close enough to defend themselves. This riot led to both Darnell and Mann being expelled from Cooley High for the rest of the school year and having to meet with the Superintendent. During this meeting, the superintendent said that Darnell would have to attend Pershing High for the following year. Being that Pershing was on the East side, Darnell instantly informed both the superintendent and his mother that he would not be attending a school on the East side when he was from the West side and would be by himself. Darnell knew that going to Pershing would be a fight everyday, and he wasn't willing to do that. His protest resulted in him being transferred to Redford High School. Darnell soon found out that Redford High was a fashion statement school and a showcase of the haves and have nots. If you didn't have the newest clothes and the freshest shoes, you would get talked about. At this point, Darnell couldn't stay up to par with everybody else, so he started skipping school. He would also skip school while his mother was at work. She would leave in the early mornings with the impression that he was going to school, but he would just stay home. He did this for quite a while before she finally found out that he had not been going.

After his mother found out that he had not been going to school, he stopped going during the day all together and tried night school. When night school did not work for him, he decided to drop out. To be honest, had Darnell stayed at Cody High, away from his old neighborhood, he probably would have graduated and become a welder because of the love he grew from welding while being there.

I want to pause right here though. Just for a second. This is where I want you to pay attention because if you skim your way through this, that is how you miss the message. Right now, we're about to expose a part of the system that's been doing its best work for quite some time. Yes, the education system. This is how the education system makes criminals out of black youth. It's called the School to Prison Pipeline and today it's much worse. Let's talk about it. Stay with me for the current facts.

> ➤ According to the Michigan ACLU, 68 percent of Michigan's prisoners identify as high school dropouts, and the odds of dropping out are even greater for Detroit's Black students as they contend with higher suspension and expulsion rates than their white counterparts.

> ➤ Nationally, according to the Department of Education civil rights data, black students are more than three times as likely to be suspended or expelled as their white peers.

> ➤ Since the 1970s, suspensions of black secondary school students have increased at 11 times the rate of white students.

> ➤ Students suspended in the 9th grade are 3x more likely to drop out of high school.

Now, I'm not providing excuses; I'm just giving the facts. One thing about numbers, they never lie. Darnell's first suspension set him up. Every time he failed a test with no academic intervention, he was set up. Everytime he was expelled, he was set up. He couldn't read the material, and not one educator caught it, they just passed him along to be the next teacher's problem. Not one educator in the system looked at his lack of presence in school and how it contributed to his disengagement from learning? They never looked for the "why". What they didn't know was that Darnell was hit by a car when he was two years old and suffered from a head injury, which contributed to his lack of focus and comprehension. He also grew very sick in first grade, and his mother had to make the decision to hold him back because of the amount of school he had missed. He was already behind. As he got older, he spent more time at home than in the classroom, he never stood a chance. It's not a coincidence that the numbers tell this same story for many other black boys. Darnell didn't hate school; he hated not knowing the information because he didn't understand it. He did whatever he could to not have to sit in that seat. And the education system let him fall through the cracks because a black boy with failing grades and a temper is a "behavioral problem" whose only solution is to kick them out.

Chapter 2

BROWN PAPER BAGS

D o you ever stop to think about your first introduction to money? And when I ask that, I don't mean seeing it. I'm not talking about when you would get a few dollars from somebody to go to the corner store and get all the snacks you wanted or the money flower you'd wear at your birthday party while you opened up the cards, hoping money would fall out. I mean, when were you introduced to money being the means of survival? See how different of a feeling you have towards money now? See, now it's not just that thing you need for your favorite bag of chips but that one thing that now makes a difference between having a roof over your head or being homeless? Let's get into the moment Darnell was first introduced to money.

Darnell's mother, Sharon spent 30 years working in the community as a social worker. That job helped her to raise her boys, put food on the table, and kept a roof over their heads. Until it didn't. After spending decades in her career, she lost her job. She then spent time trying to find another means of taking care of her family. She would have gigs here and there, but nothing that was really secure. Many employers felt she was either overqualified or not qualified at all. This left her on the verge of losing everything, including the home that she owned. The livelihood she became accustomed to, as well as her boys were flashing before all of their eyes. Until her eldest son, Derrick, took the position of head of the household. This is when you step into survival mode.

Derrick went missing. He just left. No explanation, no talking, or no questions. He just disappeared. Darnell and his mother would ask around the neighborhood, but no one could tell them where he was. Darnell and Mann went out and looked for him everywhere too. No answers. Two weeks later, he walked into the house, and before anyone could ask anything or say anything, he just pulled out two brown paper bags. Then he dumped them out, and wads of money fell on his bed, and he put the other bag away. He handed the money to his mom and said, " Pay the mortgage; this will put you ahead and use the rest for food and bills." Darnell was very familiar with their environment and what went on around them. He knew exactly how his brother was able to bring that kind of money to the table, and later on that day, he confirmed it. Derrick showed them what was in the other paper bag, and it turned out to be heroin and rocks. While he and his younger brother were not off the streets, they were still in them and aware of their surroundings. One day, Derrick took Darnell and Mann to the same house where he spent his weeks making money. It was a drug house. Derrick was able to pay his mother's mortgage by selling Heroin, and he then made it very clear to them that if he ever caught either of them at that house or doing what he was doing, it would not be good for them. They both knew that threat was one to take seriously. And they listened. However, Derrick would still just show up every time with money, taking care of the house and then some. Right then and there was when drugs and money started a toxic relationship right in front of you. See, when you begin to see money as a means of survival instead of a luxury, the things you will do to survive are endless. Because now money is seen as a scarcity. There's not enough to go around. Survival mode kicks in, and you have to do what you need to do so that life doesn't chew you up and spit you out. It's no longer about right from wrong; you're either going to eat or starve, and I didn't know too many people who would choose to starve.

Although Derrick seemed to be owning his position as Head of the Household successfully, there always comes a time when positions get changed. Whether in corporate America or the streets, in order for things to continue to run smoothly, there is always a position to be filled. One thing that we know to be consistent is that the streets only have two roads. Death or Jail. Derrick went down the road of incarceration. And just like that, Darnell and Mann get promoted to heads of the household.

Chapter 3

THE PAYCHECK

J ust like any other job, you can hold the same position and do it a different way. You can either do better or worse than the last person who held it. Both Darnell and Mann tried to maintain the position the same way they saw their older brother do; however, it didn't work out the same way. While the pressure wasn't as heavy when their brother held the position, being that things got a little better at home, Darnell still wanted to be able to pull his own weight, so when that didn't workout, Darnell decided to get his first job. He began working at Burger King.

Darnell, his younger brother, and some other friends would always take care of each other when things got hard. There would be times they would be hanging out and getting hungry, and no one had any food at the house or money to get with it. Even with his job, it still wasn't enough. Because of this, they did what they had to do to eat.

They would put their plans together to get some food. Darnell, Mann, and their friends would go to the local corner store to get the drinks, and then their sisters Dinez, Amanda, and their friends would go to the grocery store and steal the food. They would meet back at the house with chicken, steaks, sides, and even snacks, and that's how they ate for that day. This happened more times than once, and to them, they were just surviving; there was no right or wrong.

Darnell spent the whole summer picking up shifts and getting as many hours as he could. He made connections with the managers, and they knew he was the person to call if they ever needed someone to come in. He would clock in during the evening hours and wouldn't clock out until the early mornings. During that summer, there was a week in particular that he had worked the craziest hours. Picked up every shift available. He had racked up so much overtime that he just knew his next check would be more than nice. At this time, in the late 80s, the minimum wage was only $3.35. He picked up his check and could not believe the numbers he saw. After all the hours he put in that period, his paycheck was only $119. He also did not have a bank account at the time. He would get his checks cashed at the local corner store, and to do so there was a $20 fee. So there he was, after pulling all those extra hours, even pulling all nighters, just to be standing on pay day with $99 dollars in his pocket. To him, it didn't add up. Darnell was great at the job. He knew everything there was to know. He knew how to open the register, close it out, and how to make every food on the menu. He was so good at the job that they offered him an opportunity to be in the junior management program before school started back up. But, all Darnell could think about was that paycheck.

See, when money is attached to survival, your time becomes a lot more valuable. And when your normal is showing you that time is money, where do you get the patience?

So, instead of accepting the offer, he called up his younger brother, and that phone call led to another phone call, which brought Darnell back to the toxic relationship with drugs and money. This time, the drug of choice became "rock" cocaine.

Chapter 4

NO MIDDLEMEN

W hen you have something you don't know how to do but can find someone to do it, that's where a middleman comes in. Now, while Darnell and Mann were ready to bring in rock, they didn't know how to cook it themselves. Even though Derrick introduced them to it, he never walked them through it. There was a process to cook up dope. You know, in all the hood movies, that same scene that used to teach us the basics with the visual, there is a small pot of water boiling the smokey glass that has baking soda in it. You couldn't tell anybody they didn't know how to cook it up after watching their favorite hood classic. It wasn't truly that easy, though. So the best thing to do was bring in a middleman and pay them to cook it. And that is what he did. Until he realized he was being beaten at their own game. See, there was a liquid base that rock had to get to before it actually formed, and during the liquid process, the middleman would pour out a little extra on the side, and once it turned hard, he would have that extra on top of what he was being paid from them. When they realized what was happening, they learned to cook it themselves and cut out the middleman so that they didn't have to worry about being beaten.

Chapter 5

THE MOVE

———————— ꕥ ꕥ ꕥ ————————

Everything looks different when you cross state lines. Even yourself. That change in environment makes a difference. It definitely did for Darnell. That was Youngstown, Ohio, for him. He saw the opportunity to be a bigger fish in a smaller pond and took it. With Detroit being so big, there wasn't a lot of opportunity to be recognized. You could be known in your neighborhood, but it's always been level to the streets, and someone was already standing on it. In order to reach that level of celebrity and city wide notoriety, you'd have to match "Big Meech" energy. Demetrius "Big Meech" Flenory and his brother Terry "Southwest T" Flenory were the head of the Black Mafia Family "BMF," a drug trafficking and money laundering organization in the United States that started right in the city of Detroit. They had direct links to Mexican Cartels and distribution centers in Los Angeles and Atlanta. Levels. So when Darnell saw the opportunity for his own level of celebrity, he took it.

What started out as helping his family move turned into him moving himself. His mother would have described this shift as the same. She had never expected him to leave home so soon, but every phone call added time to his Youngstown visit before he eventually just told her that he and his brother Mann were finding a place together and he would be staying there. She didn't think anything of it, but they saw everything they needed to see. They asked the right questions and got all the information they needed from their stepbrother, "Dump." Dump was from Youngstown, and not only was he in the streets, but he was also using it, so if anybody knew what to do and where to set up shop, he did. After talking to him, Darnell and Mann both knew what they wanted to do. So they put their money together and made it happen. Darnell came to the table with $100, Mann matched him, and they borrowed another $100 from someone else. They took their $300 and went back to Detroit to buy a half ounce of powder. Then, they came back down to Youngstown and set up shop right in Youngstown, on the streets of Hillman and Warren.

Things took off slowly at first. They would catch whatever cars they could, and whoever got to the car first got the sale. There was also a woman who lived in the blue apartments on the corner, and she would come out to buy from them here and there too. After they got to know her more, she would let them come in and warm up when it got cold outside. Eventually, they got close enough to her and sold her the idea of paying her to set up shop inside her apartment.

While in Youngstown, they realized that Youngstown was behind in the drug game. They were a lot more fast paced in Detroit and they knew the difference. Opportunity, they knew that all they had to do was cross those state lines and things would hit differently on the other side. See, in Youngstown, the top drug being sold at this time in the late 80s was powder cocaine. It contributed to the epidemic that swept the nation during that era of time. While powder cost slightly more, you would think it was the better sale, however, it didn't create the same demand as crack cocaine. Also recognized as "rock". See, the chase was always high. Rock brought them up to their high quicker, while Powder took longer to feel. Youngstown had not yet been introduced to it. Until they were.

This process was even slower than selling the powder because they were trying to get people to buy the rock instead of the powder but like most people, they stuck to what they knew and kept buying the powder instead. So they decided to stop selling the powder all together and only offer rock. They reintroduced it by throwing specials such as 2 for $5, 2 for $10, or 3 for $12. They would throw those deals for different occasions or days, and it started working for them. Eventually, people got on board, and it started selling better than the powder did.

No one knew who they were or where they came from, but they knew where to find them to get what they wanted. Sometimes that's all you need. It wasn't long after their transition to Youngstown that they began getting to know who was who around there. They started getting closer to different families and friends as they became more familiar with the new city they were in, and that is how they met Rick. Rick had been introduced as their cousin from Cleveland, and their relationship after that kind of stuck. He would come back and forth between Cleveland and Youngstown before eventually moving to Youngstown as well. The duo started to grow a little.

Chapter 6

READY ROCK

I f it's one thing the streets know how to do, it's putting a name to a face. It's only a matter of time before you get one. No one in Youngstown really knew who they were. They pretty much showed up in the city and started making moves, and people started paying attention and began knowing them as "Them niggas from Detroit." That was all people really knew about them.

Darnell and Mann lived in an apartment across from another group of guys. The guys were really cool with Dump, and he would basically be the middleman between the two houses because no one else really knew each other. Whenever they needed to buy something, they would tell Dump, and he would take care of the transaction and take it across the street. Gradually, over time, the guys started to call them "The Ready Rock Boys" because they were the only ones selling rock at the time, and that was the only way to really identify where to get it from. Eventually, the name stuck, and other people started catching on and calling them the same thing. At this point, even though people still did not know exactly who they were, what they did know was that they were not from the city, and if you wanted rock, they were the ones to have it.

Darnell and Mann ended up buying themselves some Mazda B2200 trucks. Darnell had a black king cab, and Mann had a blue one, which he turned into a convertible by getting the top cut off. Rick also bought himself a new car which was a purple Nine Eight Oldsmobile. Those cars had become their new identifiers. People knew somewhat of who they were when they rode around the city. At this time, everyone else rode around in old used cars while Darnell, Mann, and Rick rode around in brand new custom cars.

This caused a little unintentional friction. Not everyone was very welcoming of the brothers coming and drawing attention to themselves. Not only were they drawing attention, they were making money doing it. A few more guys from Youngstown that started to stick around were Eddie, Shimmie, and Tariton, and the group grew a little more again. That name started to ring bells. From "Them Niggas from Detroit" to Ready Rock Boys.

Chapter 7

HOLLYWOOD

L et's pause for a second because we don't talk about a drug dealer's Hollywood enough. We all know once you've made it to Hollywood status, you've made your way. See, success looks different from every angle depending on where you are looking from. Let's break this down. Think about the BET awards. What's the first thing that came to your mind? The red carpet? If you were to look up the symbolism for a red carpet, you would find words like honor, prestige, high status, stars, fame, and the list goes on. Even if your first thought was the performances. You'll see that the show provides a major platform and a celebrity spotlight. This is what the streets provide for successful drug dealers. Mind you, I said successful. Success looks different depending on where you're standing. While some will think morally and say that it is wrong, the streets will roll out the red carpet. A drug dealer's Hollywood comes with fame, recognition, and access to money that most people don't get to see and access to things most people don't get to have to live in the hood. You will be respected, feared, hated, and envied, but the strongest attraction to Hollywood is that you'll be loved. We all know that there are only two roads guaranteed on the way to that kind of Hollywood. It's death or jail. But the saddest part is your inmate number, and your casket is still equal to a star on the Hollywood Walk of Fame, and the streets give them out too.

Darnell got his first Hollywood moment, and it came out of nowhere. Darnell and his sister Dinez were in the process of buying the house that they stayed in together. Darnell and Mann were trying to buy another house during this time too. They reached out to their guy from the bank and asked him to get them a list of properties being sold by the bank. He came back and gave them a list of about 30 properties that were available. Things started being put into motion. One random Sunday, the guy from the bank stopped. He never came around unannounced and definitely not on a Sunday, so this confused Darnell.

"Everything good? My sister gave you the payment, right?" He asked him.

"Yeah, that's not why I'm here. I was just around and wanted to stop by and see how y'all were doing and talk to you about something." He told him.

"Oh, yeah, everything is alright. We're good."

They continued to carry on conversation when he went on to tell Darnell, "Clean your house up. If they knew that I was telling you any of this I could lose my job."

Darnell knew exactly what he meant by telling him this and knew what he needed to do next. Even though the house that he and Dinez stayed in was not a house he sold out of, there were still drugs there. He made a phone call to have everything in the house moved out of the house. That following Tuesday made the random Sunday visit all make sense. The house had gotten raided. Darnell was just getting out of the tub and heard some noises coming from downstairs. He thought maybe it could have been Dinez and started to look around while he walked back to his room. He then started to hear footsteps coming up the stairs, and before he could turn around all the way, the police were standing at attention, telling him to get on the floor. After they got him on the floor and handcuffed, an officer named Officer Patton came into the room and slapped Darnell.

"Take these cuffs off me, and I'm going fuck you up!" Darnell yells as they are destroying everything. They continued to search the rest of the upstairs, let Darnell get some clothes on, and then took him downstairs. As he's coming down, he sees Dinez, Eddie, and a few others handcuffed as well. They searched the rest of the house and came up with nothing. Darnell's truck is in the garage, and they went on to search it. After looking through everything, they came back empty-handed again. An officer named Clark yells, "Check it again!" and sends them to re-search the vehicle. While they were still doing their search, Eddie and the guys in the room started rapping the "Fuck the Police." While this was happening, the officers came back saying they found 2 keys of powder, and that was all they needed to take everybody down.

As they are all walking out of the house in handcuffs, you would have thought the whole of Youngstown was in front of that house. Not only were the people outside, but so were the news cameras. It was like lights, camera, action!

They were all booked and awaiting arraignment. When they got arrested that day, every bondsman and lawyer was on standby waiting to see who would get the call for them. Everyone had gotten out on bail except Darnell. The bondsman that he was familiar with didn't want to touch the case because of how big it was, and with Darnell being from Detroit he thought that Darnell would run and would only allow him to make bail if he had some type of collateral. Darnell's mother offered her home as collateral as well as his girlfriend's grandmother offered both her home and the lot she owned next door; both were still denied. Darnell sat in jail for 3 weeks before reaching out to another bondsman, and Darnell bailed out the very next morning.

Darnell was willing to risk his freedom to get his Hollywood star, and he made it there. Being that young, at only 19 years old, with a name that brought that much power into the limelight, it was addicting. That's the power of "hood celebrity." They will talk about your story forever. They will remember your name. You will be a legend in the streets for making it to a drug dealer's Hollywood. Who's to say that's not success? Where are they standing?

Chapter 8

TWO ADDICTS

The definition of an addict is a person who can not stop doing or using something, which means you can still be an addict even if you aren't the user. So there's really no difference between the drug dealer and the drug user. Both are addicted to a high and neither one can stop. Darnell was addicted to the lifestyle, and it brought him a high. Once he crossed those state lines and created a name for himself, he was never the same. It's kind of like that Money Mitch moment in the movie "Paid in Full," where he expresses the love he gets from the streets. He says, "If I leave, will the fans still love me?" That's the power of the streets. All love ain't good love, but it's still love, and we all want it. And when it becomes all you know, you'll do anything to keep feeling that love. You literally crave it. That was his relationship to selling drugs. It brought too much love to him.

Just like the addict that's using, there's usually a rock bottom they hit before they decide it's time to stop. But Darnell had gotten so deep into it even he didn't see his way out. There would even be times when he had hit a drought, and just like an addict, he needed to scratch that itch. It wasn't even about the money anymore; he just needed to sell drugs, and he was willing to pay any price to get it. During his drought, to make everything straight, he started to short people on the product, making it more baking powder than cocaine. He would turn 4 quarter ounces into 5. So not only is he making his money back and more of a profit, but he's making the satisfying itch longer.

Darnell's mother was concerned about his addiction. She always had thoughts in her head about what could happen if her son didn't get out of this lifestyle. She wondered where his rock bottom would come from. What would get him to give up the streets? What would save him? But Darnell was already addicted. He was so far gone that there wasn't anything that could pull him out. Even when he had his first son. Darnell's mother knew this was it. You couldn't tell her that this wouldn't change him and bring him out of it all. While the fairytale story of having your first kid being the reason you change your life for the better is warm and fuzzy, that was not the case here; he didn't clean at that moment. There was no epiphany. The addiction still won.

Chapter 9

THE HOOD SCHOLAR

N o one loses in win-win situations. Darnell found himself in one with a guy named Andre. Andre played football together with Shimmie and Tariton back in high school and would come around from time to time. He was never too much in the streets; he just hung around and kicked it from time to time. Andre had been trying to go back to college and was telling Darnell everything he needed to do to get back in. Darnell wanted to help him out, so he let Andre use one of his cars to drive up to Bowling Green and register for classes. Andre had been counting on some money his father had left him. He was going to use that money to pay for school. As it got closer to the semester starting, Andre was getting all his paperwork together so that he could start taking classes, and when the time came to pay his tuition, he found out that his mother had taken the money and spent it herself, leaving him with nothing. When Darnell found this out, he wanted to help him out.

Darnell knew that Andre wasn't really in the streets like everyone else was and was really trying to better himself, and he didn't want to change that for him. He came up with an agreement that would help both of them. It was meant to keep Andre out of the streets and still put some money in his pockets. Darnell thought about the house he was using and how much money it was making daily. Darnell was already looking to remove himself from having to be at the house so much, so he told Andre to make sure they always had stuff there to sell and that there was always food. All he had to do was pick up the money and drop off whatever was needed for the house, and Darnell would pay him every week. That was the arrangement, and it worked until it didn't.

Darnell started to get a feeling about the movement at the house and felt like it was being watched. Something didn't feel right to him, and he started to get ahead of whatever he was feeling. By this time, Darnell had just had another run-in with the police a couple of months ago. He was in the car with one of his friends, and they stopped at a car shop. It had been real hot on the southside, and the TASC force was raiding all up and down the hill and riding around. When they pulled into the parking lot of the car shop, Darnell takes off running. He never heard footsteps behind him or saw them chasing him, but he called his lawyer the next day to let him know what had happened. One of the officers had found drugs in the parking lot and said that they had Darnell's fingerprints on them. A month later, an indictment came out. Not only was Darnell dealing with this new case over his head, but he was still fighting his Hollywood case. So Darnell's paranoia was taking over because he knew he couldn't afford to be caught up in anything else. Whatever feeling Darnell had about that house, he made sure to listen to his gut. He pulled up to the house and told Andre what to do.

"I'm about to shut this down; it's getting too hot around here. Just go ahead" He told him.

By this time, the few others that Darnell had working at the house he had already told to get out of there, and all that was left was Andre. Andre told Darnell he wanted to stay and sell the rest of the products that they didn't sell before they left. Darnell was against it and told to just leave the house and let it go. Unfortunately, Andre didn't listen and Darnell's gut feeling was proved to be right.

Later on that night, the house was raided, and Andre was still there and was caught with everything that was in the house and arrested. Darnell finds out and immediately calls down to the bondsmen and lets them know he will be bonding Andre out. The very next day, someone goes over to the house and when they come across a warrant, they call Darnell. When Darnell gets there he finds out that the warrant is for the house and it is put in his name. At this point, Darnell is confused because his name isn't on anything that has to do with the house, so how can they issue the warrant in his name? He calls his lawyer and lets him know everything that has just happened. His lawyer knew that his name being on the warrant put him in an even worse spot than before, so he did everything he could to fix it. In the meantime, Andre finally got his day in court, came home with no jail time and was given 12 months non-showable probation. It would be safe to say that Andre and Darnell picked back up where they left off, but that wasn't the case. They pretty much separated and didn't hang around each other anymore after that.

Chapter 10

THE LONGEST WEEK EVER

━━━━━━━━━━━━━━━ ୬୧୬୧ ━━━━━━━━━━━━━━━

N ot all beautiful moments last forever. Some are very short-lived and you don't always get the chance to take it all in before it's gone. One of Darnell's short-lived, beautiful moments was on May 11, 1993. On this day, he welcomed his daughter Asia into the world. Asia was born prematurely, which made this moment that much more special to him. Becoming a father again was such a highlighted time for him, and what was to come days after that he did not see coming. On May 16th, Darnell was leaving a local bar and walking to his car to go home. A car drove past, and as he was getting in his car, he heard two shots go off. He kneeled down trying to get to cover. As he began to come back up, he could feel something running down his face. He went to touch his face and saw that it was blood. Darnell had been shot in the face! He started to use his shirt to cover up his face. The bullet had hit him right under his nose and came out through his right nostril. He could feel somebody grabbing his arm, and he started to pull away from them realizing he had been shot in his arm too and could not move it. The bullet had gone in and out of his shoulder. *"Nobody touch me! Stop touching me!"* All he could remember after that was his friend Eddie helping him into the car and speeding to the hospital. "I can't die right now. My baby is still in the hospital. Not now." That was all he kept telling himself. As he laid on someone's lap on the way to the hospital, the only thing he could think about was that Asia had still been in the ICU, and he did not get the chance to bring her home yet.

The police finally arrived. One of the officers on duty, Darnell had recognized. He could remember a few years back in his late teens, that same office had pulled him over. During that stop, the officer said to him, "You won't live to see your 21st birthday." Fast forward back to the night of the shooting at the hospital, that same officer was trying to get a statement from Darnell and told him, "It looks like you cheated death." This caused a back and forth between Darnell and the officer, causing the doctor to intervene. "Are you done questioning him? It's time to leave." The officers agreed and proceeded to leave. The doctor didn't understand why this specific officer was being so hostile to him. He felt at that moment Darnell was the victim; he was the one who had been shot. What was the issue? As the doctor began to examine Darnell's face again, you could hear commotion right outside the door. Darnell could hear yelling, "That's my brother, I want to see my brother! Yall just brought him in!" He recognized the voice and realized it was Shimmie trying to get to him. Moments later, Shimmie walks in and stands by his bedside. They both look at each other, and Darnell can see tears forming in Shimmie's eyes. At that moment, the first thought that came to Darnell's mind was that something was wrong with his face, and he would need to get plastic surgery.

Darnell was released from the hospital the same night. They stitched his nose, patched his shoulder, and discharged him. You would think that was all enough for the week. But it only got worse a couple days later. Things start to get just a little more interesting, ending this week with a bang. Let's introduce everybody to Jackie. While Jackie is new to you all, she is not new to Darnell. She's been around quite a while actually. Jackie is Rick's mother. She and Darnell had a system; it worked for them, and they had their own code. She would send that code to his beeper. It would be her address, and after her address would be a number. That number would represent how much she wanted. They had an understanding that if he did not show up to her in 15 minutes, that meant he was either out of it or out of town.

On this specific day, Jackie kept paging him. Even after the 15-minute system, She continued to page him back to back. At this time, Darnell was with his sister getting ready to take her somewhere, so they took a detour to stop by Jackie's and answer the page. When Darnell pulled up to her house, he already felt like something wasn't right. He had recently heard a rumor about Jackie setting someone up to get robbed or setting them up with the police. It hadn't been confirmed yet, but the way she was blowing his beeper up that day, knowing this rumor was out there, made him uneasy. Usually, when going to Jackie's house, he would pull into the driveway, but on this specific day, he parked across the street. He told his sister before getting out of the car, "If you see any niggas coming out or the police, just drive off." As he walked up the driveway, he saw a car with a familiar looking woman in it. He had seen her at Jackie's a few times but didn't really know who she was. As he looks in the car, she waves for him to get inside. He gets inside the car, and she asks, "You got something '"' "Nah, Jackie is in there" he responds. She replies, "No, I'm waiting on her, so you ain't got nothin'?" Darnells snaps at her, "I just told you I ain't got nothin'," and exits the car to walk back to his. As he's walking back towards his car, someone yells, "Darnell, I'm gone blow your head off!" Darnell then ducks his head and starts running across the street, just hoping his sister did what he told her and pulled off. He then starts running through backyards and jumping fences until he gets to a familiar house and bangs on the door. They let him in. He then calls Eddie to come and pick him up. He starts to look out the window, and as he's looking, he sees his car ride by with his sister on the passenger side. At this point, Darnell doesn't know what's going on. Once Eddie picks him up, he takes him to a secure location, things seem to have died down, and Darnell gets the rest of the story from his sister later on that night.

When Darnell finally talks to her, he finds out that the men who came out of the house were actually the police. She heard the man yelling about blowing his head off, so instead of pulling off as he told her, she got down in the car, thinking there would be shooting. When she lifted her head, she was met with men at her car door and guns in her face telling her to get out of the car. When she got out of the car, the officers searched it and found nothing. After searching the car, one of the officers took her to their grandfather's house. As she was getting out of the car, the officer began searching the car again. This time, he found a gun. The officer picks it up and says "Well, look what I found." She says, "What? That's yours? 'The officer laughs and replies "No, it's your brothers." At this point, their grandfather comes outside and asks what is going on. She then screams, "They are trying to plant a gun on Darnell!" He then asks the officers if his grand daughter is under arrest? They replied with "No." "So take the car or leave it, but get out of my yard." He tells them. The officer then got back into the car and drove away.

The next morning Darnell gets up and calls his lawyer to let him know what happened. His lawyer then goes downtown to get ahead of it and they have no idea what he is talking about or what he was there for. When he asked them what was going on with his client's car, they looked up the information and said "There's nothing holding it or any charges pending, the car is free to be picked up."

Chapter 11

THE COLDEST SUMMER

———— ༄ ༄ ༄ ————

There have always been two paths that can be guaranteed down the road of being a drug dealer. It's either death or jail. There are not many success stories that come from this lifestyle. Darnell was well on his way to going down one of them, and for a while it looked like death was just staring him in the face everyday. At this time in the 90s, Youngstown was considered to be the murder capital, and the numbers continued to rise throughout the decade. There were 492 homicides in the city, averaging about 50 homicides per year, with the Southside accounting for over 200 of them. You can imagine that this was a traumatic time to be in the streets. Constantly watching over your shoulders because you never knew what could happen. Here today, gone tomorrow, and that was almost a reality for Darnell.

One night, Darnell had just got back in from a skate connection. He and his then girlfriend Tahnee had pulled up to the house around the same time. The next day, they were supposed to be moving into a new place, so they were planning to pack that night. Darnell started watching TV in the living room, and she joined him shortly after. With Sportscenter playing on the TV, Darnell finds out that Buffalo has beaten the Cowboys and instantly calls Rick to rub it in his face as usual. The next few seconds after that took a drastic turn, and it seemed to happen simultaneously fast. Tahnee had gotten up and began to walk into the other room, and Darnell started to hear barking, which was followed by a gunshot. While he had been sitting there, what he didn't know was that two men had walked on the porch coming from each side. He saw a burst of wind through the curtain on the window and before he knew it, a bullet hit him in the chest like someone punched him. It happened so fast that he could not see who or what was happening. The way that the living room was set up, the TV was in the corner, and there were three windows on each side of the front door. The couches were on each side of the living room. He dove to the floor and pulled himself to the other couch so that he could be out of sight and the shots just continued coming in from the windows on each side. He made sure not to make a sound so that they would think they got him. The shots went on for at least 5 minutes. When they finally came to a stop, Darnell began to scream out to Tahnee, "I'm hit! I'm hit! Come and call the ambulance!" The only phone they had was in the living room with him, but she was too afraid of what she would see if she came in there and all Darnell could see was black. "I can't go in there! I can't." It took her a little time to finally come in, and when she did, all she could do was scream and hold him as she saw the blood coming out of his chest. She tried to call the ambulance, but for some reason the line was busy. She hangs up and dials someone on their speed dial, who turns out to be her aunt. She goes on to tell her aunt what has happened, and her aunt tries to call herself.

While at home, Rick's police scanner goes off, saying that there had been a shooting on Gaither. Darnell and Tahnee were the only young black couple on that street, and Rick knew that. At that moment, he knew that it had to be Darnell, so he called him instantly. Tahnee answers the phone confirming that it was their house, and tells him what has happened, and then Rick goes on to call Mann, who was in Detroit at the time.

A few minutes later two police officers arrived at the door. One of them, Darnell recognized. He was the cousin of someone he knew. That officer began talking to him trying to keep him conscious until the paramedics arrived. Shortly after, the paramedics came rushing in and all Darnell could remember was passing out as soon as they began to examine him. When Darnell regained consciousness, he was in ICU at the Southside Hospital and the first person he saw was his mother sitting in the chair on the side of his bed. "Ma, I'm alright." he told her. "How are you alright layin 'up here in a hospital bed? You ain't alright!" was her response. He had been shot in his chest, in and out of both of his legs, and grazed in his upper left arm, elbow, and side. He was hit a total of 6 times.

Darnell's mother would have described this period of time as one of the most devastating summers for her. She did not know whether or not her son would make it through it. She constantly worried about getting phone calls that he would be gone. She had gotten to the point of feeling numb. She knew there was nothing she could say or do that would get him out of the streets; she could only pray and hope she didn't lose him. She had always heard about women whose sons had been shot, and even with all that Darnell had been there before, it still never registered to her that someone could walk up on the porch and shoot hers. This time was her wake up call moment. But it still was not his.

That summer of 93 'went just like that. There were back to back shootouts. You couldn't see your enemies without making a move. It was a kill-or-be-killed mentality going on back then, and there was a warzone going on in Youngstown.

Chapter 12

I GOTTA OUT DATE

———————— ᔐ ᖆᔐ ᖇ ————————

January 19, 1994. This day was the start of something that changed Darnell's life forever. Darnell got a call that Mann had been caught in a raid along with Carlos and Andre. After hanging up he rushed over to his sister Dinez's house to wait for Mann's call. A few hours passed and they finally got a call from him, and nobody expected what came next. "The county jail is overcrowded, they ain't really get nothin 'but a little drugs and some guns. They said they were supposed to be letting me go but the feds just put a hold on me." is what Mann said on the other line. Now nothing makes sense. Since when did the feds put hold on somebody over some guns? Something ain't right. After hanging up with him Darnell started trying to put the pieces together. As the day went on, people gradually came by the house that day including Curt near the end of the night. They all sat around drinking and talking. Now Dinez lived in an up and down duplex. She lived on the top. The people staying below her had control over the temperature so at times it would either be cold or hot. On that night, it was super hot. While everyone is kicking it, one of Dinez's friends notices that Curt still has his coat on and says something about it. "Why are you still sitting over there with that coat on?" "Bitch fuck you." he responds on his way out. Darnell didn't know why Curt had left so quickly, he had only been there for a little. All he knows is that when he took a look around he was long gone and he didn't come back that night.

The next morning, Darnell was woken up by banging on the door. At this time Darnell is the only one up in the house. His sister was sleeping in the other room and her 3 month old daughter and little cousin were sleeping on the floor in the living room. Darnell got up to look through the door and it looked like TASC and Fed cars and vans parked outside. By the time he goes to step away from the door, it gets kicked in. The officers rushed in yelling, "GET ON THE FLOOR! GET ON THE FLOOR!" One of the officers then hit Darnell in the back of the head causing him to fall on the floor. "Watch the baby, watch the baby!" He yells back at them. Just as he says it, one of the officers steps on her and his sister starts to go crazy as she comes out of the room and hears her baby crying.

The officers are instructing Darnell to tell her to calm down and get her under control. 'What you want me to do when y'all just stepped on her baby. She ain't worried about nothing else" They cuffed him, picked him up off the floor and took him into his sister's room. The officers began asking him, "You got something you want to tell us? You're looking at 25 years if you don't cooperate," Darnell replies " Tell you what? You mean tellin 'on somebody? I ain't telling y'all nothin', I gotta out date."

After the force finished their raid and secured the location. The Feds came in after to finish it up. Darnell was taken on that day and It wasn't too long after that Rick, BB and Mike Donley had gotten picked up later too.

Darnell was ready to do whatever time he would be given because he knew at the end of the day, he had an out date and was coming home. They took them all straight to Cleveland after being picked up. On their way to Cleveland, the judge was notified that they would be arriving and all things at the courthouse stopped. There was already a trial going on and they stopped it right in the middle to prepare for their arrival. When arriving at the courthouse Darnell met a man named Scoob During processing. "Y'all the Ready Rock Boys? They just stopped my trial cause 'yall was coming in." Darnell did not respond, he just gave him a look. "You got any priors?" he asked. "Yeah I got two." Darnell responded. "Oh yeah, you lookin at life, that's what they are trying to give me." Darnell responded with another look and left it alone.

Chapter 13

THE SECRET INDICTMENT

⊃ ၆ ၆ ⊂

After they were done being processed at the courthouse, they were then transferred to Painsville, Oh. As they were all sitting in the holding cell waiting to go upstairs, they started trying to replay the past two days to figure out what happened and how they'd all got jammed up like this. The pieces weren't being put together and it didn't make any sense. They began calling them all one by one until they all ended up in different rooms and on different floors. When Darnell finally gets called, he gets assigned to the 5th floor. When he got into his room, he couldn't stop thinking about what Scoob had told him at the courthouse. Out of all the times he had any run-ins with the law, it was never anything like this. He had never been that far, this time felt real different.

The next day, Darnell finally got phone privileges. One of the phone calls that hit differently for him was the conversation with his mother. She said something that at first rubbed him the wrong way. She told him "I can sleep at night." At first Darnell didn't understand how she could say that. It wasn't until later on he realized what she meant. She didn't have to worry about those phone calls of her son being shot, dead or in jail anymore, she knew exactly where he was. He started to think to himself and realized how much stress he had been putting her through and it had him feeling some type of way. He never realized how his mother felt about the life he was living. It sat with him.

A couple days later, there was their bond hearing.

Actually, hold on, It might be time for another pause right here to see if we all get the same image. Just visualize for a second. It's 5 in the morning and they are woken up for court. They rounded up everyone who had court and put them on the elevator to go down for processing. At this time, they were shackled, handcuffed and then put in a single file line as they made their way to the bus to be transported to court. When they arrived at the courthouse their shackles and handcuffs were removed and they were taken straight to a holding cell to wait for them to be called for their turn. On their way up to court they were handcuffed again and instructed to face backwards in the elevator. Okay, did you see anything? Did it remind you of something? Did you think about slavery? Okay, that's all. Anyway, back to the bond hearing…

When everyone arrived at the courthouse, as they sat in processing getting ready for court they tried again to see if anyone had gathered what was going on by this time. Still no answers. Going into Court, Darnell finally meets his public defender, Debra Hughes, and the conversation lasts for about 2-3 minutes. In that small conversation, Darnell finds out this is a secret federal indictment and not only is he facing 5 counts but it's the United States v. Darnell Walker as he is the head of the whole indictment. He starts to think to himself , "Okay, they got me for 5 counts; they gone give me 5 years for each of em 'and run em 'concurrent." In his mind, that's what's getting him the 25 years they told him about. He was okay with that fate because in his mind, "I gotta out date" was playing over and over. As the hearing proceeded, the judge denied them all bail on the basis of considering them a flight risk. Actually, that's not true, the only one who was able to get a bond was BB. Which seemed odd, because they were all in the same boat. How can they be considered a flight and he wasn't? Or how could they even be considered flight risk without the capabilities to leave the county? Yeah, they could have left the state but how far would they get? No one had a passport. It just keeps getting more confusing as more things unravel. After the hearing they were taken back to Painesville. Darnell left court with no real answers and still no clarity.

The next day Darnell gets a visit from Debra. However, she's not by herself, she has a man with her. "I can't handle your case, this is Donald Krosin and he's your new attorney." Donald then starts talking to him and explaining that he is a good trial lawyer which catches Darnell off guard. "I'm not tryna go to trial. I know I got 5 counts against me, they said I'm looking at 25 years. So that's what? 5 years for each count? See if you can get me a plea deal and run em 'all concurrent." he tells him. "This is not the state. It's not that easy." he starts trying to explain to Darnell again that he is a good trial lawyer. Donald starts to try and reassure Darnell with his experience and letting him know that before mandatory minimums, he was beating all of his cases. He agreed to try and get Darnell a plea deal but warned him it wouldn't be anything small while reminding him again that this was not the state. At this time, the Federal system had a 98% conviction rate. Numbers don't lie; nothing about that number said take it to trial. His new public defender thought otherwise.

A few days later was the plea hearing. At this point Darnell is feeling like he has to take an overnight crash course on law as Donald is trying to explain to him his right to a speedy trial. He had no idea what he was talking about. All he knew was that he did not want to go to trial, anything outside of that was just foreign to him. His lawyer encouraged him to waive his rights so he did. He thought that was working in his favor because to him, he never wanted to go to trial so he felt he had more time to fight against it. But in reality he just gave the system all the time they wanted to hold him before giving him his day in court.

The following day, Darnell got another visit from Donald, and what came from it he never saw coming. This was where Darnell found out the 25-year luxury sentence he banked on may not happen. Initially, the assistant US Attorney, Linda Betzer, only knew of 1 of Darnell's prior convictions. However, she came across the second one. Finding this out gave her the green light to threaten to file for Information 851, which stated that those 2 prior convictions could enhance his sentencing into a mandatory life sentence if Darnell continued to refuse to cooperate.

Chapter 14

FIRST 9 MONTHS

———————— ⊃⟆⟆⌐ ————————

The more the case started to unravel, the heavier things got. At that point everything was pointing to Darnell; in the eyes of the government, he was the head of it all, and it was so much stacked against him. He started to realize he was about to be up for the fight of his life. He already felt like he couldn't win, and the only thing he knew how to do was just fight, but he didn't know how many people he would be fighting against.

The day Donald brought him his actual indictment sent Darnell in a loop. His head was spinning. He had gone from mastering the streets to crash courses in law and politics. As he broke his charges down to him, it all seemed like a foreign language. The only charges he really understood were distribution and one of the gun charges. The 2nd gun charge seemed odd because there was only one gun on record. Being that Darnell was a convicted felon, he was not supposed to carry. Okay, that makes sense. However, they also charged him with use or carry during a drug transaction. Now, an even bigger piece to this puzzle was the gun they were charging him with. Let's pause and rewind for a second. Do you remember during the longest week ever, when Darnell had a run in with the police at Jackie's house and they claimed to find a gun in the car the second time they searched? Yes, that day. Do you also remember him letting his lawyer know what happened just for his lawyer to go to the station and see what charges were being brought on Darnell, and no one knew what he was talking about? Exactly. That gun is this gun, and it has made its way around. Now, Darnell was supposed to be on his way to deliver drugs to Jackie which brought about the 2nd gun charge of using and carrying a gun during a drug transaction and it carried a mandatory minimum of 5 years. It was all beginning to circle back around.

There were so many pieces to this puzzle, and everytime the piece got put together, the bigger the puzzle got. "......." The exact words on the indictment. Conspiracy. It is defined as an agreement between two or more persons to commit a crime in the future. As Krosin broke down the conspiracy charge to him, he made sure to let Darnell know that conspiracy is easy to prove but hard to defend. That charge is so broad, and any type of conversation can turn into conspiracy just by one simple sentence; it could have been anything that brought this charge about, and Darnell had no idea what it could be. "Looking at this list, who do you think will cooperate?" Krosin asks Darnell about everyone else on the indictment. As Darnell scanned the list, one person he had a feeling about was Andre, and he couldn't see anyone taking that step. It all just seemed like everything was closing in on him. The only thing he was feeling at this was frustration, confusion, and hopelessness, and it only got worse when Krosin started sending evidence in.

Chapter 15

BETRAYAL, DISLOYALTY, HURT

Y ou always feel like your people are your people, and they'll always have your back. Because in your mind, you will always have theirs. That wasn't the case for Darnell. As time went on, things got weird with a few people, and that was just something else on the list of things he never saw coming. One thing Darnell did see coming and was absolutely right about was Andre cooperating. It had been so obvious. He was there with them one day, and the next, he was transferred out to a different county jail, and it didn't take a rocket science to figure out why. That's how the system works, once you start cooperating they'll ask if you fear for your life, and of course Andre said yes, so they moved him. Even though Darnell knew this would be the case with Andre, he just didn't know exactly what was said yet.

Being that they were on different floors, they didn't get a chance to talk much. On the 5th floor were Darnell, Rick, and Mann, but on the 2nd floor were Carlos and Mike Donley. For some reason, Carlos got moved around and ended up on the 4th floor. That move ended up putting another piece of the puzzle together. See, rec was held on the 4th floor. It's one of the hours they gave to the inmates outside of their assigned pods. They split the pods up and sent them to their specific part of rec based on their assigned days. They'd either be sent to the gym or outside, which wasn't really outside. It was in the middle of the jail with a gated ceiling you could see out of. Either way, they didn't have a choice between the two.

No one knew that Carlos had gotten moved until one day while Mann was at rec, Carlos knocked on the window to talk. After rec was over, he let Darnell know about the move. The next time Darnell's pod was scheduled for the outside rec, he knocked on Carlos 'room window to talk with him.

"What's up, they offer you a plea?" Carlos asks.

"Nah, they ain't offer me nothin'; I'm suiting up and going to trial" he yells back.

"You goin 'to trial? Man, they got pictures and all that type of stuff." Carlos responds with big, surprised eyes. His whole energy took a shift.

Darnell knew at that moment and said to himself, "Nah, not him too." He just didn't want to believe that they got to him.

After rec was over, they went back to their pods. Scoob pulled Darnell to the side. He had overheard the conversation at rec between him and Carlos.

"Man, I know that's yo guy and all or whatever he is to you, but he tellin'" He told him.

"Dang, I saw it too," Darnell replied.

It was already in the back of his head, but Scoob peeping it was just extra confirmation that what he thought was right. After talking to Scoob, he knocked on the door, called for Mann, and told him what had just happened. Mann told him not to talk about it and that they'd see about it the next day at rec.

The next day comes, and they're called for rec again. For some reason, Darnell's pod ends up outside again. He and Scoob walk over to Carlos 'window to talk with him and the room is completely empty. When they realize that everything is gone they both give each other a look. Meanwhile somebody ends up walking past the room and Scoob knocks on the window. The guy walks over to the window and he asks, "Aye what happened to the guy that was in this room?" He responds with a motion like somebody was picking up a crate and moving it. Which could only mean he got moved just like Andre. Darnell and Scoob knew exactly what that meant. See, once Carlos found out that Darnell was actually going to trial, he knew that his statement would come out and made sure to be transferred out before it did.

Shortly after statements started to roll in. Krosin started sending Darnell the information as he got it, a little more was unraveled than the obvious. That wasn't the end of the singing that went on. Now he's finding out not only what Andre and Carlos said, but everyone else who made a statement too. Along with their statements were two more. Rick's mother Jackie and his aunt were amongst those documents. I guess you can say Jackie was expected. I mean being that she did set him up that day, it wasn't too surprising that she also had to make a statement.. However, Jackie's sister Wanda is another blow he didn't see coming because where did she come from? He didn't understand her position. She didn't even have any real information, just speculation but that was enough for them. Darnell and Rick spent some time staying with her and while staying there, their beepers kept going off and they did a lot of moving around. That is what she told them and she made sure to point some fingers Darnell's way. But why? What was the need for her statement? She wasn't facing anything or even a part of the indictment at all. These were the thoughts rolling through Darnell's mind.

It was like the list of names went on and on. Darnell also got the list of people who would be taking the stand and a couple names stood out to him. Lorenzo and Scottie Reynolds. He could recall the time he sold to Lorenzo but he couldn't put his finger on what Scottie had to do with this indictment at all let alone what he would say. What did he even know?

At this point, Darnell is feeling like everybody is against him. What did he do to make anyone willing to take a stand on him like this? "Why me?" is all he could think about. The 3 words he used to describe this time for him was betrayal, disloyalty and hurt.

Chapter 16

JURY OF MY PEERS

A jury of your peers is a carefully selected group of people from the same community who could be considered an equal and will unbiasedly be able to hear the case fairly and it is a constitutional right. For Darnell, he didn't understand how a group of law abiding and career driven citizens could be his peers. The definition of your peers is considered to be a person who is equal to another in abilities, qualifications, age, background, and social status. So, how could they be his equal? Not to mention if the jury should be unbiased, why were they choosing people from the same community they were on trial for destroying. They've watched the news, they've heard the stories, and an opinion of the Ready Rock Boys has already been formed. In Darnell's mind he would never get the jury of his peers and whoever they chose definitely wasn't it.

During the process of elimination in selecting the jury one of the questions the potential jurors were asked was "Can you serve as a juror on this case?". One of the men replied. "No, I think they're all guilty." He was struck from the jury and could not continue. Another person who was struck happened to be BB's uncle and he let them know that they were related and that's how that process worked. They were asked a series of questions to make sure there was no bias. "Do you know anyone in this case? Has you or your family been a victim of drug abuse or violence?, etc." By the end of it all a jury was selected and surprisingly it was a predominately black jury. Usually many would say that would have been said to be a good thing, but in this case, that didn't matter.

Chapter 17

THE STAND

E ven though Darnell had received the statements from Krosin, things didn't become crystal clear until it was time to get on the stand. He's in the fight of his life; it's him versus everybody, and it wasn't just the system he had to be worried about. He was getting hit from all sides. One of the clearest pictures that was finally painted on that stand was where this secret indictment even came from. The testimony from Officer Patton felt like a movie. He was one of the leading officers in Darnell's case and took the court to the very beginning. At this point, it isn't new information that Curt was an informant. What no one knew is what made him do it.

Curt had been caught in a raid at someone's house. While the police were raiding the property, they found him on the landing by the basement, but what they also found were drugs down in the basement after finding him and charged him with them. While Curt was at a court hearing, he and Darnell ran into each other as Darnell was dealing with another case himself. They talked for a little, and Darnell asked how was everything with his case going. "Oh, it's cool, I got a lawyer out in Cleveland, I'm gonna be good." They end their conversation and Darnell walks away. As he was leaving, Officer Patton was coming out of the probation department on the other side. As Patton walks passed, Curt went to stop him and asked "Do you want the Ready Rock Boys? I can get them for you." While Patton didn't take him seriously at the time, he still gave Curt his card and told him to give him a call. Curt gave him a call, and at first Patton didn't take him seriously until he set up the first buy with Mann. Once he realized that Curt was actually going to do what he said, he started building a case, another buy was set up, and the next one went to Darnell. Anytime Curt was around, it was just like any other day with him. No one suspected he couldn't be trusted, so no one tightened up, which only made things easier for him. This not only led to all of Curt's charges being dropped from his case, but in Krosin's mind Curt was being paid for his services, but that was never proven.

The more Patton built his case, the more he tried to get the Feds to pick it up. At the time, they wanted nothing to do with the case, and it stayed at a state level. Until it didn't. All this time, Darnell had been wondering why the government was coming for them. What did they do so bad that caused a federal indictment this big? Come to find out, even though it never truly came out in open court, the timeline was loud and clear. A young girl was killed that previous summer, and Shimmie and Eddie were falsely accused of her murder. Ironically, soon after, the Feds decided to pick up the Ready Rock Boys case tying it to gun violence, and just like that, the case finally went from State to Federal.

Another missing piece gathered on the stand was Wanda's reason. Her role in making a statement left Darnell confused about her position, but it soon was revealed. She was applying to be a police officer and was denied the opportunity because of her relationship with them. However, they made her a deal. If she provided them with information on the Ready Rock Boys, they would allow her to join the police force. So she took her opportunity.

During the Trial, Dinez was subpoenaed to testify and was supposed to appear the following day to take the stand. Darnell ended up calling her later that day, and she let him know about her subpoena. Dinez had a plan to lie in order to be in favor of him, however, Darnell did not agree. He told her to tell the truth because he knew that on the day they were questioning her about was the day that Jackie set him up and whatever she would say could not hurt him in any way and that was the truth. She never saw him with a gun or drugs. She was only riding with him to Jackie's house that day. There was no reason to lie about anything. Although she told the truth, the Jury still didn't believe her. In their eyes, she was just trying to help her brother.

Trial brought everything out. Darnell finally got his answers as to why he saw some unexpected names on the list. Even the few he thought had nothing to do with the indictment at all. Lorenzo, being one of them, was actually brought on the case as a connection to BB. Rick and BB spent a lot of time together, so Lorenzo was used to making sales from him instead of Curt because Curt had no real history with BB. In the process of trying to get BB caught up, Darnell came over to BB's house at a time when Lorenzo was also there. Rick needed to make a run home; however, Darnell had Rick's car blocked in and let Rick use his car instead of moving to let him out. What they didn't know at the time was that Lorenzo was wired up and was followed to BB's house that day. When Rick left to go to his house, the police were still watching BB's and left to follow Rick. Being that he used Darnell's car that day, the assistant US attorney used that as fuel to push the conspiracy narrative of all of them working together for organized crime. Lorenzo's piece of the puzzle wrapped quite a few people up in this indictment, such as Mike Donley and Tracy. He would come to the house to buy it, and instead of BB being there to sell it to him, he would get it from someone else who just so happened to be at the house.

One day, Tariton called Mann and asked if he had anything for him. Mann, at the time did not, but a guy he was with named Carlos said that he did, and they set up a buy. They were at Dinez's house and found a ride to go make the sale. When they got there, Lorenzo turned out to be the person who was actually buying, and he got in the car. Lorenzo pulled out the money and Carlos robbed him and kicked him out of the car. It wasn't long after the police caught up to them, but only Mann was able to get away. What they didn't know was how the police were able to catch up to them so fast at the time. But it was all coming out when Lorenzo got kicked out of the car; he ran away and as he was running, he was also giving a description of the car because yet again, he was wired, and the police were already following him.

Between Curt and Lorenzo, they were able to get 28 tapes' worth of evidence. They wore wires during private conversations and drug transactions and even tried catching phone calls too. Each time they set up a buy from someone, they would buy more than the last one so that they could have evidence of a larger amount of the drugs. It was all strategic, and the feds kept it going long enough to be able to hold decades of time over everyone's head to see if they would fold.

As for Scottie Reynolds, to the assistant US attorney's office, he was a key connection to a bigger fish. Scottie was kind of like an uncle to Tariton. He was a friend of his father and when he died, Scottie made sure to look out for Tariton as much as he could. However, Scottie spent some time in and out of prison himself. There was a guy named Vince, who he had met while in the halfway house, and they became well-known associates afterward. Well, Vince and Tariton got acquainted and decided to take a trip to New York together. They never made it because they ended up getting caught in New Jersey with over $26,000 in the midst of the investigation. The Assistant US Attorney saw this as a way to use Vince to testify against Tariton to connect him, Scottie, and the Ready Rock Boys to Vince's father. His father was currently locked up for 200 Keys at this time, and connecting them all to him would have made it look as if Scottie was their connection and his drugs came from Vince's father.

Not only did they put Vince on the stand, they also put Scottie up there too. Knowing that Scottie was going to testify didn't sit well with Tariton. Before court started that day, Tariton had a nice bit of choice words for him and the only thing that Scottie said to him was that he couldn't say too much but for Tariton to wait and see what he would do on the stand. He knew he had given drugs to Tariton before but he also knew that with his two strikes and pending violation, he couldn't afford to be connected to the indicted at all with his priors otherwise, he'd be on trial facing life too. So Scottie said something on the stand that helped everybody. When asked about the drugs Tariton had gotten from him, he said that they were a gift. He had only given Tariton 9 ounces, which was nothing to him, and he didn't expect anything back. As a matter of fact he said the amount of drugs he gave him was equal to the gas he put in his Benz. Because Tariton never paid for the drugs and he didn't owe anything to Scottie, it wasn't considered to be a drug deal. There was no connection. This helped everybody because they couldn't connect the Ready Rock Boys to a criminal organization, and it got Scottie out of being added to the indictment himself. It's safe to say Tariton changed his views on Scottie's cooperation and understood what had just happened.

See, in the game of The Stand, everybody benefits. You give to get. Everyone who took the stand benefited in some kind of way. Those weren't the only pieces to the puzzle getting put together. There were plenty more. Lorenzo got his driving under suspension tickets taken care of, Andre got a shortened sentence in his deal, and Jackie got charges dropped. There were so many of their own people taking the stand to testify that at the end of one of the trial days, the U.S. Marshall said, "Damn, who else in y'all family gone come and testify against y'all?" The comment he made couldn't have made more sense for what happened in that courtroom.

Darnell felt like everyone was against him even more, and he would have never seen things unravel the way they had. But does anybody really? Many times, people get wrapped up in the streets and there is always a crowd in the process. There are people to party with, laugh with, sell with, and spend with. But when you hit that wall and it starts closing in on you, not too many people are coming to your rescue. If anything, they're most likely coming to their own defense so that they don't hit a closing wall. When it's you or them, seldom people will pick you. It's two types of winning in the streets. Only one really gets the real recognition. That's when you make it to Hollywood. That's the one everyone hears about the most. No one really talks about the other side of winning. When you give somebody else up to save yourself. People probably won't look at you the same, but is it not still a win? See while it doesn't get you the same "Hollywood Star" from the streets, the stand is still a part of the game even though everyone doesn't play that way. Darnell certainly didn't, but he's only one player, and because everyone played the game their way, he was convicted of all charges.

Chapter 18

LIFE

―――――――――― ⟩⟨⟩⟨ ――――――――――

After the trial was over, another waiting game started for Darnell to be sentenced. He didn't know what to think. So much had come out in that courtroom, and he didn't know what position it really put him in. The wait for finding out his fate was longer than expected; months continued passing by, and a lot of what was going on outside of the county walls had a small part in his long wait.

During his waiting game to be sentenced, the Million Man March had aired on TV and Darnell tuned in. The Million Man March was a large civil rights demonstration in Washington DC, organized by black religious and community leaders with the help of Louis Farrakhan, a leader of the Nation of Islam. Many prominent leaders gave a speech at the March such as Martin Luther King III, Maya Angelou, Rosa Parks, Jesse Jackson, and more. During one of the many speeches that day, Farrakhan made sure to criticize the harsh sentencing for nonviolent offenses such as the 100:1 sentencing disparity between crack cocaine offenses compared to powder cocaine offenses. The 100:1 disparity affected black men more than any other race as they accounted for 88.3% of those convicted of federal crack offenses. At this time, Congress was two weeks away from the deadline to make a decision on the request to change the 100:1 to a 1:1 that was voted on and submitted by the Sentencing Commission.

Let's break down the Sentencing Commission for a second. In 1984, Congress eliminated parole for federal crimes and started the Sentencing Commission and mandatory minimums. The commision controlled the sentencing guidelines. The sentencing guidelines consisted of 6 different categories based on criminal history. Category 1 least serious and is usually first time offenders Category IV is the most serious and made up of those with a serious criminal record. The charges of the offender that are presented in the pre-sentencing report determine the level that offender is on. Each category is made up of 43 levels and depending on the seriousness of the crime, points could be added or taken away to get a final determination of the offender's level. The category and level each determined how many months an offender was sentenced to. Pay attention to the chart below to get a better understanding of the sentencing guidelines.

Insert Guideline chart.

Being that the 100:1 disparity was one of the determining factors in Darnell's sentencing, both Krosin and the assistant US attorney agreed on postponing Darnell's sentencing hearing until Congress made a decision. A week after the Million Man March was over, it was like Congress finally flexed its power, denying the sentencing commission that ignited the "1995 Crack Riots" throughout the Bureau of Prisons.

After Congress denied the sentencing commission, a date was finally set for Darnell's sentencing. At this point, knowing so many people had turned on him and how much time he was facing, he couldn't do anything but think about ways he could fight for his children no matter what the outcome would be. Knowing that he was facing life, he also knew and felt that the charges he faced did not warrant a life sentence. It wasn't possible. In his mind, that was being used as a scare tactic to get him to cooperate and he refused. His main focus always came back to his children and how his situation would affect them. Darnell was 3 weeks away from his sentencing, and he came across a newspaper article from USA Today. It was about the United States vs. Bailey federal case's ruling on 924c, which was Darnell's second gun charge. The language of the charge was very vague, but what the Supreme Court did clear up was that it had to be proven that the gun was either used, carried, or both while committing a crime. Neither of the two was proven about Darnell during trial, so as soon as he could, he got right on the phone to call Krosin. Krosin let him know that he was already aware of the case and he filed a motion to get the charge vacated and Darnell's sentencing was postponed again.

As the weeks go by, Darnell speaks to his lawyer the day before his sentencing. Krosin is telling him the worst and best case scenarios. At this time, it is around the holidays and Krosin says "Hopefully the judge had a good Christmas and decided to sentence you to 20 years instead of life, but it could also be appealed by the Assistant US Attorney." The conversation with Krosin left Darnell both hopeful and doubtful but more doubtful than anything because he just didn't think that it would happen to him like that.

Sentencing day is finally here. Things started off on a good note. The judge granted Darnell's motion to dismiss the gun charge that held him to a mandatory 5 years. However, that seemed to be the only wish granted that day because things got tricky after that because the sentencing guidelines that Darnell was on didn't work in his favor, and they made sure to throw the book at him. Darnell was charged with conspiracy, which could carry up to life , however his conspiracy charge was an 841(b)(1)(b), which only carried 5-40 years. Darnell was a Category 3 on the guidelines and started at level 32. However, the judge and assistant US Attorney gave Darnell 6 more points. He was given 2 points for the dismissed gun charge and 4 points for being considered a leader. This put Darnell at level 38. Now if you refer to the sentencing guidelines, Darnell should have been sentenced to 24-30 years. However, something different happened that day. The system did its best work. The assistant attorney filed an 851, which was an informative notice that they requested an enhanced sentence on Darnell's charges. This is why the assistant US attorney wanted to bring Darnell's 2 previous convictions into this case because once they were able to get an amount of at least 50 grams or more, it triggered the 3rd conviction to warrant a mandatory life sentence, and that took him off the sentencing guidelines.

They needed 50 grams or more on one count and technically they did not have it, but that didn't mean they couldn't work around how to charge him with it. Out of the 28 tapes that were admitted as evidence, Darnell was only on 4 of them. Out of the 4 tapes, he was only able to be distinctly heard on 2 of them. Because of this, he was never charged with those extra two drug sales, but they still used the tapes to influence his sentencing because he should have been sentenced on each count separately instead they added them all together and charged him with 50 grams or more.

"Even though what you were doing was wrong, it doesn't warrant the time that I have to give you. If it was up to me, I would give you time served, but my hands are tied." Said the judge before giving Darnell his sentence. At this time, Darnell had already been locked up for 23 months. However, because of the sentencing guidelines and the enhanced charges, there was nothing the judge could do. The 851 was just what they needed to do it all, and Darnell was sentenced to mandatory life and 5 years concurrently for his gun charge.

None of this made sense. Darnell was the only one on the indictment who received a mandatory life sentence without the possibility of parole. They made him the head of the indictment and used him as an example. Darnell wasn't just the only person to receive a life sentence on the indictment, he was the only person to ever receive a life sentence for a federal drug case in Youngstown. When this whole thing started, Darnell was willing to do his time and come home. He knew as long as he had an out date, he would be okay. Instead, his fighting for his life turned into a life sentence he was never supposed to get.

Chapter 19

NO APPEALS

It never truly hit Darnell that he had just been sentenced to spend the rest of his life in prison. Darnell could not stop thinking about the judge walking off the bench without reading him his rights. He knew something wasn't right about the look on the judge's face after the assistant US attorney reminded him to do so. Krosin let Darnell know that had the judge continued to walk off the bench, it would have automatically reversed his sentencing and Darnell would have had another opportunity to get in front of a judge and maybe even build a better case. Darnell couldn't help but think that maybe things could have been different.

On the day he was sentenced he told everyone in the courtroom that if he ever made it back home, he would build up whatever community he was in and start his business. In his mind, he was going to try anything he could to keep his word. His lawyer let him know that his first order of business was to make sure he filed a notice of appeal within the first 30 days to try to get a lighter sentence, and he went for it. Luckily, he did tell him because Darnell had no idea he was already put on a clock for his freedom. Once he put in his filing, the next part of the process was the waiting game for a briefing date. One of the things working in Darnell's favor was the fact that he was in the 6th circuit court of appeals. In the 6th circuit it's almost automatic that you get the opportunity to present oral arguments in front of three judges. In most circuits, you have to argue for that option. Darnell has one case that he felt so strongly about. He knew that the United States vs. Winston's case would give him the reversal to get a new sentence. He would have bet his life that the case would free him. Darnell was so anxious to get a decision on his appeal that it felt like time was standing still. Everything around him just stopped as if he had put his whole world on pause. It was just a waiting game for that letter in the mail.

When that letter finally came in the mail about two years had passed. That letter was the beginning of the wind being knocked out of him. It wasn't what Darnell was expecting, nor what he was hoping for. His direct appeal had been denied. Once a direct appeal is denied, you have the option to go a step further, appeal the decision, and present it to the full 6th circuit. This meant that all the judges in the circuit would now hear the case. Darnell made sure he went for it. He was determined to keep the fight going to get the judge's decision overturned. Another waiting game that led to another door being closed in his face because this appeal had been denied too. Darnell still wasn't defeated. He kept going, trying for the Supreme Court next. See, the Supreme Court will have thousands of cases that would come across the desk of the solicitor general but very make it through to be heard. Darnell's case had been denied getting passed the desk, which was yet another denial of his appeal. You would think that was just enough to make Darnell stop trying; however, he didn't. After being denied by the Supreme Court, he had exactly 1 year from the day of the denial to file a 2255 motion. Which is a legal motion filed by the inmate to correct a federal sentence, stating the reason why the decision should be overturned. After another waiting game, that motion led to yet another denial. Darnell continued filing again and again. He had filed just about every motion you could think of. He filed so many motions that the judge wrote at the bottom of the cover sheet, saying, "Do not file another thing in my court again unless you get permission from the 6th circuit." But to Darnell, his freedom was more important than an annoyed judge, so he continued to file. He had gotten so many denials that he didn't even want to open the letters anymore because he knew they would say denied. He had stopped reading them and would skip right to the part of the letter that told him whether or not his motion was granted or denied.

Darnell started losing hope the more he was denied. It started setting in each time that he might really spend the rest of his life in prison. He felt desperate and stressed out. He felt like he knew he had a good case and that he had the right issues to argue he just needed someone to hear it and do the right thing. He was discouraged and it all just made him second guess everything he had been thinking about his sentencing. His mother tried her best to keep his spirits up the more it got broken. She would speak positivity over him and let him know something good was still possible. That kept him sane as much as it could, but it was getting harder and harder to keep hope.

Chapter 20

HURT, ANGRY AND DESTROYED

———— ༄ ༄ ༄ ————

The more nos Darnell got, the more reality started sitting in for him. He began thinking he might be there alot longer than he thought. After coming to the realization that it was time to get comfortable, his true survival instincts started kicking in. He made it his business to stay to himself and wasn't really interested in making too many new friends. The only person he knew and associated with was Scoob. This was an adjustment for him, but it worked. He didn't smile much or talk a lot. He didn't walk around with a chip on his shoulder either, he just had an anti-social demeanor.

Darnell found peace in working out. He and Scoob would work out together on the daily. He also started going to the library often, and reading became another outlet for him. Once he started getting into a routine, things started to settle down more. Something that did stand out to Darnell was that it did seem to be less stressful than being in the county. See, in the county, you're facing trial, you don't know your fate, there's a revolving door of drug addicts coming in over the weekend, and there's people facing a few months in the county crying about their time while you have a life sentence hanging over your head and none of it made the time go by faster. Once he was really adapted to the prison environment, it was different, there were a lot more people in his situation than not, there were plenty of people doing real time and everyone around just did what they had to do to survive. He also started to catch on that everyone did their time their way. You just had to make a choice. Darnell didn't get caught in any of it. He didn't join a gang, he wasn't Muslim, he didn't join a Christian organization, none of it. When you're in prison you're constantly asked to be a part of these groups and asked to come around. Darnell decided to walk alone with his own two feet and never had an interest in being a part of anyone's group. The most connecting Darnell eventually started to do, outside of his connection to Scoob, was with guys from Detroit and Ohio. They just always seemed to gravitate to each other naturally, being that someone always knew someone else and made the connections happen. For the most part, Darnell made a habit to mind his business and keep his head down.

Darnell later on started to gravitate to the "old heads" in the prison. He began learning from them and became interested in black history. He started to read a lot more and talked to different men in the Nation of Islam, the Sunni Community, and the Moors Science Temple of America which led him to attend an event called the "Book Bizzare" at the chapel, which was created by a guy named Jahad. Jahad was a black panther who was accused of trying to break another panther out of jail. He went to the head of each group and brought all 3 Muslim communities together for this event. They all respect him enough to be a part of this event despite their differences. There would be different topics being discussed, skits, and in between breaks there would be tables set up from each community with books that people would be able to sign out. They all referred Darnell to the right books and even later checked in to make sure he read them. This became a part of Darnell's routine, and he would fill up on books. The more people he talked to, the more directions they would point him in to get the right books to read.

Darnell had really started developing his new normal, and he worked for him. Attending the Book Bizzare opened Darnell's mind to so much and gave him a whole mindset shift. Even just seeing the way Jahad carried himself around the prison made Darnell almost join the Muslim community himself. Although he still found his own path to do his time his own way, he started to find peace in his new normal.

As much as Darnell got used to his new normal, he never expected to have to adapt to yet another one so quickly. Darnell gets an unexpected visit from his children's mother. He had not been expecting a visit from his kids until the weekend, and she was by herself, this was weird because at that time she wasn't really coming to see him without the kids. Darnell walks out, sees her and is completely confused, asking where the kids are. As they hug and take a seat, she stares at him and realizes the news he is about to hear is coming from her first.

"Oh my God. You don't know." She says.

"Know what?" Darnell responds. At this point, he's even more confused. "Whatever it is, just tell me."

Before she can even get the words out, she starts to cry.

"Derrick's dead."

Darnell couldn't do anything but look at her in disbelief. Saying nothing. Tears began forming in his eyes. She began telling him more about what happened and the more she spoke the more Darnell sat in disbelief about what he was hearing. This was a pain he had never felt before, nor did he see it coming. When the visit was over, as he walked by to his room, he kept replaying a conversation he had recently with a guy, and he can remember telling him how he had never experienced the hurt of losing something that close to him. He couldn't fathom how he could have met that reality so quickly after.

The first thing Darnell did when he got back to his block was go and call his mother. He had no idea what he would even say to her. When he got his mother on the phone she asked why he hadn't called yesterday. Darnell's mother had called the prison multiple times, telling them to give Darnell the message about Derrick, but no one ever told him.

After finding out the news and speaking with his mother, Darnell went into a state of anger. He became so angry that he didn't even trust himself. Knowing that, he told a few people he trusted to keep an eye on him because he wasn't himself. He started learning a lot more about himself, and he realized it was hard to control that type of anger. It was a different kind of hurt for him. What he did know was he couldn't afford to get into it with anybody because of his anger. One small argument can always lead to something bigger in the environment he was in, and that is why he wanted to be looked after.

Darnell didn't attempt to go to Derrick's funeral. He knew it would be slim and didn't want to deal with it or put the burden on someone else while his family was already having a hard time. Instead, he wrote a letter that his son would read at the funeral on his behalf. Darnell and his mother never spoke about Derrick afterward. It was like that thing in the background they didn't speak on.

Darnell picked up another outlet some time after. He had gotten himself a journal and started writing. He started with writing down definitions to expand his vocabulary. Darnell had been reading so much that whenever he couldn't pronounce a word or didn't know what it meant, he would write it in his journal and define it. It wasn't long after that Darnell started to write his daily thoughts down too. He went from using his journal to keep track of words to using his journal as a release.

"Thursday, March 5, 2005,

This is the official starting day for my journal. I should have started this years ago. There were a lot of important things and events that happened to me. I can remember the time when I cried for 2 hours when I felt the hurt and pain from DeJae. (July 16, 1998). Also, when Derrick died July 20, 2000) July was not a good month for me. Now I have a chance to add something like this everyday. I want to just see how it goes; who knows, maybe one day my children can write a book on this or just understand what I went through during this hard time. I do understand one day maybe shorter than after but these are my thoughts."

Darnell's journal really became the best release for him. Whenever he felt like he had no one to turn to or that no one would understand him, he would put the pen to the paper and let it out.

"*Saturday, April 2, 2005,*

Today is just like any other day and it's not over with. Once in a while I'll feel alone, like there's no one in this world but me. Today is that day, like when I try to reach out to someone they're not home or I want to talk to someone but I don't know how to get in touch with them. The one person I do want to talk to, I haven't been able to for about 5 years now. I used to always count on Derrick no matter what, But I know my brother is always there understanding exactly what I'm going through, my pain, my struggle, my love. I do pray to one day make my life complete, to have a wife, another child and to live life to the fullest. Last night I had a dream that seemed so real. I received a letter in the mail about my sentence being reduced or going home but I knew for sure I was going back to court and possibly home. The best thing about it, I had a chance to let Dejae and Asia read it on a visit. So the last thing I remembered was holding my hand over my eyes and crying. What a peaceful feeling..."

"*Thursday, April 28, 2005,*

Today was just any other day. During and leaving prison changes a person physically, mentally and personally. Once you leave here things will never be the same. You can't trust anyone or depend on anyone. You will never look at family and friends the same again. They will never understand what you went through or going through, no one will. All this is from being frustrated and disappointed how everyone is me and not helping me. But once I 'm out I will survive like I always do. This shit hurts but I have to and will deal with it. I have to remember some of Derrick's words, 'Rely on NO one.' And that's what's going on now, I can 't rely on no one, I will survive. Peace and Loyalty..."

"Friday, May 13, 2005,

Today was just like any other day. I don't know how the conversation got started but it was the hardest thing. I had to tell a woman who already lost one of her sons to a bullet and now she knows that she might lose another to bars. Me telling my mama that it's a possibility that I could be here the rest of my life. After 11 years, 3 months and 3 weeks that life in the Feds means just that. Telling her that really hurts but I had to tell the truth without sugar coating anything. All my cries out for help might be too late. I don't know what tomorrow will bring but I 'll deal with it when it comes. Peace and Loyalty..."

"Thursday, October 03, 2005,

I can not believe it has been 10 years. I remember being in the county jail when the Million Man March was just starting. October 15, 1995, now the 10 year anniversary is here and I 'm still locked up. What brought this on is this article I read in USA Today about this girl, her father, and her brother. It's very touching. I can relate to alot, because I 'm living it. Even those I love, my brother and father, I have my mama and children, brothers and sisters. Not being there for Dejae and Asia really hurts. I do feel like Breea C. Willingham's pain. I've been going through this for 11 years and 9 months now. I pray that one day, I'll be released from my bondage and chains. Until that day, Peace and Loyalty..."

Chapter 21

STOP THE CLOCK

T ime never stops. No matter how long you're standing still, time will keep on moving around you. That's what it felt like for Darnell to watch his kids grow behind those walls. It was like watching them from a distance but not being able to be a part of it. He can't recall ever going long periods of time without seeing them, being that they always came to visit and pictures helped, but he always noticed changes in them as time went by. He could see them getting taller, voices changing, and even DeJae growing a little mustache. It became something he could feel at times. He knew he was missing something but couldn't pinpoint exactly what it was, but he felt it. There was one specific visit with DeJae that left an imprint on Darnell. The visits with his kids always went good as they always did, but when it was time to go there was a shift. As he looked at DeJae he could just sense that something was wrong. Whatever it was just felt so heavy on him. When he hugged him, Darnell felt like he had absorbed all his pain from him. He just wanted to take all his pain away at that moment because he could feel it too. They didn't speak about it but he could tell they both knew. This day crushed him. He walked back to his unit with his head down until he got to his room. He laid down, put his head on the pillow and just cried.

It still didn't really hit him about him missing pivotal moments until memorable events and graduating from those milestone grades started happening. Those were moments that he knew he would have been a part of. It hit him even harder when Asia went to prom. All he could think about was that some little knuckle head was taking his baby to the prom, and he couldn't be there. One year Asia went to the Cinderella Ball. A local fundraiser competition in the area for young black girls. Asia won the crown that year and all he could remember was seeing pictures of her in this white ball gown as beautiful as she could be and he was not there to be a part of that moment with her. When she graduated and moved to Akron for college, he thought about how he would be there for her move in a day to help her unpack and share her first day on campus with her. One moment he missed that broke him was while Asia was in her early 20s. She has suffered from the loss of her first child as a still born. Darnell wanted to be there for her more than ever. He wanted to be able to hold his baby while she held hers in her arms. This was the one time he felt he truly let her down, not being able to be there for her at such a traumatic time in her life. They never talked about it but Darnells feels that moment will always stick with him. Because she really needed him and he wasn't there, he only blamed himself.

Another pivotal moment he could recall was DeJae making the decision to join the airforce. Darnell didn't want him to go and was against it, but after talking to DeJae more, he became fully supportive, knowing that DeJae was making a good decision for himself. The fact that he had the opportunity to travel around the world was something he wanted for his son, and that experience could never be taken from him. He had been to Italy, Croatia, and South Korea, and in those moments, he would think of his life being surrounded by cement while his son was able to travel from country to country and that was enough for him.

Aside from just trying to be there for them as much as he could during phone calls and visits, disciplining them behind those walls wasn't any easier. He had to have some tough love conversations with both DeJae and Asia. He made it his business to sit both of them down to let them know being a part of the streets was not an option for them. He let them know then and there that if he ever got wind of them doing any of it, he'd have to kill them himself. As he was giving them his word Asia seemed to be in the clouds as if it didn't really apply to her, and he made sure to let her know he was talking to her just as much as DeJae because women got caught up in the game, too. That wasn't the first or the last time he had to put them both in their place about the same thing. One day their mom overheard DeJae calling Asia and one of her friends a "bitch". She let him know instantly that she was telling his dad about it, and she did just that. On the next visit Darnell asked DeJae,

"You think your momma is a bitch? You think your grandma is a bitch?"

"No." He replied.

"So why do you call your sister one? That's your flesh and blood; you don't do anything like that. Now I want you to apologize to your sister, her friend, your momma, and everybody else."

Not too long after that, he had to have the same conversation with Asia about the word "Bitch". She had been talking to some boy at the time and went on to say, "That's my nigga, and I'm his bitch." When Darnell heard about this he was fuming and made sure Asia knew it.

"Didn't we just go through this with your brother calling you a bitch, and you went sit up here and let this knucklehead call you one?" He says to her.

"Ah, dad, he wasn't calling me one," she replies.

"But you said it. You ain't nobody's bitch. Never disrespect yourself like that or let nobody else do it, and on top of that, you also know how I feel about that "N" word. So, those are two things right there I don't agree with. We not doing that, and if this little dude looks at you like that, leave em alone."

Darnell tried to make sure in any visit, he left nothing unsaid with them so that they always knew where he stood on whatever situation had come about at that time and tried to make sure he didn't loosen his grip on them as best he could.

Trying to raise your kids and be there for them behind bars is nothing easy. There's so much that can be missed. It's like trying to squeeze weeks, months, and years of parenting into seconds of phone calls, minutes of letters, and a few hours' worth of monitored visits. Darnell finally realized how much of it was all his fault. Once he had kids, he should have made sure it was all about them, and he didn't. It would be normal to say, "well, he was young" at the time. Darnell doesn't charge it to his age; he charges it to the fact that he was selfish and missed out on watching his kids grow outside of the walls of the prison, which was what he got in return.

Chapter 22

GRANTED

⁓ ᏶ ᏶ ᏶ ⁓

Good news always spreads. Something major happened in the world, and everyone was talking about it. It was 2014, and President Barack Obama's administration announced the "Clemency Initiative," which encouraged non-violent inmates to petition to have their sentences commuted or reduced. When Darnell heard about this, he went to a guy named Tommy Walker to hear his thoughts on this. Tommy was really into law and loved keeping up on new cases and staying educated on current events. He told Darnell he should file for it because he had a good case. This was still conflicting for Darnell because he felt like he was still in the "fighting" stage of trying to exhaust all of his options, and at this point, he didn't feel like he had done that. He had never stopped putting in motions. He wanted Clemency to be the very last resort before he went for it, and he didn't feel like he was ready yet. As time went on, the more information he got about clemency the more interested he became. Darnell started looking into the qualifications more and checking off the boxes he knew he had. In order to be granted clemency, you had to have served at least 10 years, check. You could not have any serious infractions; he had a couple but he still didn't think it would be a problem because they were light infractions. You could not have been in a gang, check. Even though they tried to say that the Ready Rock Boys were a gang on trial, they were never charged with it. Once Darnell checked off all the things he qualified for, a lawyer from the public defender's office the named Jeff Laserous reached out to him and told him he would be a good candidate and that there was a motion through the public defender's office to see if they would be able to handle it. Months had gone by, and Darnell had still not heard back from Jeff on the status of the motion. When he finally heard back, he found out that the chief judge had denied the motion, stating that the public defender's office was already handling other things federally and could not take on anymore. After getting denied, Jeff went around to 5 different law firms to see if they could take on the clemency cases pro bono for Darnell and all the other inmates he had on his list. It became another waiting game. Ulmer & Berne, a large firm based in Cleveland, Ohio, ended up picking up his case. Darnell was talking to another inmate about it and told them that he had hoped that whatever lawyer came from that firm would be a young white woman. He said he wanted this because he knew that she would do everything she could for his case in order to prove herself. Not only did he get what he had hoped for, he got two young white women to take his case. Their names were Allison "Aly" Terrell and Linda Delacourt Summers. Even though he was happy about getting what he wanted, there was a small issue in the matter. They were civil lawyers and had never practiced criminal law before. Darnell luckily knew everything he needed to know about his case and he was a lot more prepared and knowledgeable on case laws and procedures than he was at 24. This helped out alot. There were so many steps to being granted clemency. They had to put in a little information at a time and if what was given for that step was accepted, they were granted to continue to the next step. Each step got your case closer to being on the president's desk.

Darnell was still not convinced in the process at this time. Even though he was doing his part and he was interested, he still wasn't fully on board with this being the solution for him because, in his eyes, he wasn't going to get it and was looking forward to a different way out. Darnell had been banking on Congress to make the Fair Sentencing Act retroactive, which would reduce the sentencing disparity between crack and powder cocaine from 100:1, which Darnell was held to during his sentencing, to 18:1. Making it retroactive meant that Darnell would be eligible for a reduced sentence and he couldn't wait for it to pass through Congress.

In the meantime, Darnell still kept himself updated on what was happening with the clemency route for others. There was an organization called F.A.M.M, which stood for "Families Against Mandatory Minimums". This organization was founded by Julie Stewart, whose brother received a mandatory minimum for selling weed. She created the organization to challenge mandatory minimums and advocate for criminal justice reform. At this time, FAAM acted as a community bulletin board and would post updates and information concerning clemency by sending newsletters through email. Although Darnell didn't see clemency as his way out, he still kept himself up to date on what was going on with it. He would check his email for the FAAM newsletter to see the list of names that had everyone who had been granted clemency. Everyone has gotten familiar with the process too. They knew that if someone got called down to the counselor's office, it had to be clemency. They wouldn't call you down for bad news, so everyone knew that was a sign that something good was happening.

"Tuesday, August 30, 2016

Well, President Obama is at it again today he did 111. Just one day after short of four weeks 111 more clemencies were granted and mine was not one of them. But as long as I don't get a denial next week, I am good for another month. The newsletter said worthy inmates will get clemency as long as they are put on his desk until the last day he is in office. I just pray my name is one of them called before he leaves. It is still winding down, and I'm waiting for my name to be called. Peace and loyalty..."

"Thursday, October 6, 2016

Okay, down to 104 days left in office, and President Obama did another 102. No I was not on it but I pray it will be before he leaves office in 104 days. It should be getting close because the last time Did the clemency last month he also denied 2227 people. Regardless what happens I should be coming up, but I pray, and everyone else prays that it will be a good notice. Until then, Peace and Loyalty...

"*Friday, November 4, 2016*

Countdown continues, 75 days to go, before President Obama leaves office. Today was a surprise to me that he did 72 more, that's 170 in eight days. I hope and pray that my day is soon, I get a little anxious, and that leads to impatience. Dejae helped me out with that beforehand. Just praying I'm next, time will tell, I must be patient. Peace and loyalty..."

"*Monday, November 14, 2016,*

The countdown continues, no President Obama has not done any more clemency yet. But he has 65 days left until his last day in office. With Trump being the president-elect, no one knows what he's going to do. So I pray that I'll be home to see for myself. The next entry in this journal I hope I will be writing about getting clemency, hopefully soon. This week, next week, I'm just praying that my name will be called. Peace and loyalty..."

"*Tuesday, November 22, 2016*

Countdown continues, President Obama did 79 more petitions, and they say that brings his count to over 1000 people. With 57 days left, I was not called again. I just know and hope it will be the next time for sure. Until then, I will be praying as always. It could be me next week, or next month. I just hope I'll be on that list. Peace and loyalty...

"The case manager wants to see you down at the office at 2:30pm," says one of the COs walking by. Darnell took the blanket off his bed and put it over the window. Everything around Darnell paused, including his breathing. He just couldn't catch his breath and his eyes got bloodshot red.

He went over to the sink to throw some water on his face and calm himself down. It was the longest wait of his life just watching the clock, waiting for his time to go to the office. President Obama only had 31 days left in office and if he left before you got a decision, that was it. The next president coming in wasn't going to pick up where he left off. That's all Darnell could think about.

When he gets to the counselors office, he sits down and waits to be called. As he's sitting there, a guy he knows walks past and sees him. He asks Darnell,

"Man, what you doing in here?"

"I don't know yet." he replied.

"Yes, you do. You don't be up in these people's faces like that, what are you doing?"

They both laugh. The guy takes a pause as if he's thinking and says "Ahhhh, this is it man!" before he walks out. Darnell knew what he meant by that but until he got the official word, he wasn't getting his hopes up too much. Even though he felt like this was his time too. As he's sitting there waiting, the phone finally rings and the call is for him. When he got on the phone, he immediately knew from the excitement of his lawyers 'voices. Aly immediately told him. "Darnell, I am so happy for you, they granted your clemency!"

THE WHITE HOUSE
WASHINGTON

December 19, 2016

Mr. Darnell L. Walker
Lewisburg USP
2400 Robert F. Miller Drive
Lewisburg, Pennsylvania 17837

Dear Darnell,

I wanted to personally inform you that I am granting your application for commutation.

The power to grant pardons and clemency is one of the most profound authorities granted to the President of the United States. It embodies the basic belief in our democracy that people deserve a second chance after having made a mistake in their lives that led to a conviction under our laws. Thousands of individuals have applied for commutation, and only a fraction of these applications are approved.

I am granting your application because you have demonstrated the potential to turn your life around. My decision to commute your sentence will not result in your immediate release, and you will be required to serve additional time to reflect the seriousness of your offense. I understand you may be pleased by the commutation grant but disappointed with the remaining period you will have to serve. It is up to you to make the most of your remaining time in federal custody -- to take advantage of the educational and vocational programming offered so that you have the tools you need to succeed in your second chance. It will not be easy, and you will confront many who doubt people with criminal records can change.

But remember that you have the capacity to make good choices. By doing so, you will affect not only your own life, but those close to you. You will also influence, through your example, the possibility that others in your circumstances get their own second chance in the future.

I believe in your ability to prove the doubters wrong, and change your life for the better. So good luck, and Godspeed.

Sincerely,

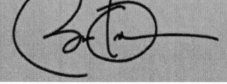

> "*Monday, December 19, 2016*
>
> *Today I was granted clemency, as time was running out. President Obama only has 31 days left in office. I was afraid I was going to get left behind. But when the C.O came to tell me I had to go to the office, I knew that was my call. Well, I prayed it was my car and it was. I no longer have a life sentence, I woke up with it but now I'm going to sleep with 2 1/2 years left. Thank God our prayers were answered. Now, I'll be able to get on with my life. The saga still goes on... Peace and loyalty...*"

Darnell is still in awe. He can't believe his sentence had been reduced and he would be home in just 36 months. It was real, and it was happening. As soon as Darnell made it back to his block, he started making calls to let everybody know the good news. He had just talked to his mom, Mann, and DeJae and he gave them the news first. One of the last things he told DeJae was that if he called him again before that following Friday, it meant that it was happening. He calls DeJae in the middle of his driving, and he can't believe what Darnell is telling him. He had to pull over to control his excitement that his dad was finally coming home. Darnell felt like he kept catching everyone while they were driving. When he called his Aunt Chrissy, she immediately burst out in tears, and Darnell had to yell at her to pull over because she was so emotional. Darnell had told everyone to keep it all under wraps until he told Asia that she was at work and he couldn't get in touch with her. He didn't want her to find out from anybody other than him. She was the last call of the day, and it was hard for everybody to keep it together. But once he finally told her, the delivery of the good news was complete, and reality really set in that he was coming home.

Darnell still had about 3 years left, but it didn't bother him; he wasn't doing life anymore. Once his sentence was reduced, it required him to be transferred to another prison, being that his security level had dropped so heavily. Once he was transferred, it was a total culture shock for him. He had spent the past 20 years behind a wall and never had to go outside for anything unless he wanted to. At the lower-level prison, everything was outside, and he had no choice on whether or not he wanted to go out there. If he wanted to use the phone, go to the gym, use the computer, wash clothes, or do anything else, he had to go outside to do it. To get to any other place in the prison, you had to walk outside. The prison he was transferred to was in Minnesota, so you can imagine how going outside during the winter was for inmates during that time. It definitely took some getting used to. But that's where he spent 2 years of his ending sentence, and for the last year, he was to be transferred to the halfway house. He never had to do his last year in the halfway house because something happened. Remember back when he thought Clemency would never happen for him and was banking on the Fair Sentencing Act to go retroactive? Well, in December of 2018, it finally did, and at this time, Darnell still had 13 months left, and he was in his last month at the prison before he would be getting transferred to the halfway house. On March 1st 2019, Darnell received a call from Claire Cahoon, an attorney from the public defender's office. She said that she had been reviewing his case and let him know he may be eligible for immediate release and that he should put in a motion to try. Even though she said she didn't want him to get his hopes, Darnell had been denied so many times before that one more wouldn't hurt, so he told her to go for it. However, he didn't see him getting it because someone he knew also filed, and they were basically told that they were blessed with clemency already and should be grateful. During his conversation with Clair, he found out that Aly and Claire were actually classmates, so he pointed her in Aly's direction to get everything else she needed to know about his case. Within the next couple of days, the motion was put in, and she let him know he would hear back from her on whether or not his motion was granted.

The next thing to do was wait. Initially, the assistant US attorney's office wasn't in agreement to grant the motion. There was some pushback coming from them. However, the judge was on board. After a couple of weeks going by without hearing anything back from Claire, Darnell started setting his mind on getting ready for the halfway house, but he still made sure to check his email and call his mother to see if she knew anything. He never told her that he had filed, but he knew that she would know if something had been granted before he would. On Friday, March 15th, he checked his email and called his mom, but nothing came of it. Saturday, he did it again. Nothing. On Sunday, when he spoke to his mom, she told him he was granted immediate release and was coming home. He knew what his mother was saying was true because there was no other way she would have known about the motion. What he didn't know was that on Friday, the judge had already signed off everything. Things escalated quickly, he had only put the motion in two weeks ago. He was never expected to be really coming home so soon with a year still hanging over him. Monday morning he got a call from his caseworker to give him the official news and he was officially a completely free man by 3pm that day.

Chapter 23

AFTER LIFE

⌐꜀ꙮꙮ꜁

Darnell's release got put in much quicker than expected, and even though he had been waiting for this moment for the past 25 years, he was unprepared. His immediate release caused him and his family to make halftime adjustments to how he would be getting home. Once he was officially released, he was still in Minnesota. They put him in a van and dropped him off at a gas station. They let him know the time the shuttle bus would be coming and that he needed to make sure he was on it. The shuttle bus took him downtown, and he was given a piece of paper with directions that told him how to get to the Greyhound bus station. Darnell pulled out the map to see which direction he needed to be going. As he is trying to read the map, he sees two women talking and goes to ask them if they know how to get to Greyhound. One of the women points him in the right direction and tells him where to go. On his way there, he passes up a store and goes in to buy a phone. He got one that needed the minute put on it. After he bought the phone, he tried to load it up with minutes but he couldn't figure it out, and there was no one around to help him. When he finally gets on the bus, he sees this girl who looks like she would know how to load up his phone and decides to sit by her. As they are sitting there, he sparks up some conversation, lets her know a little about his situation, and asks if she could help with the phone. She tried to help him out and figure it out for him, but she couldn't do it either. Even though she couldn't figure it out, she put her number in the phone and told him to keep her in the loop on what he was doing from time to time. As they come to a bus stop, he sees a younger guy on a bench sleep. He got off and wanted to wake him up to see if he could help him with the phone, but he changed his mind as soon as he thought about being left. He didn't want to miss the bus when he already didn't know where he was going, so he got back on the bus, and as he was going back to his seat, he saw another young guy waking up out of his sleep and went straight to ask him to put the minutes on his phone. He woke all the way up and was able to help Darnell out with the phone. Darnell couldn't wait to make a call; he had not talked to anybody since Friday. Little did he know, the phone was still not working. At this point, he doesn't know what's wrong with the phone. The minute we were loaded up, what was the problem. He didn't go to sleep, and when he woke back up, it was 6 am, and they were at the bus stop in Chicago. He went to try the phone again and found out it needed wifi. He had no idea what Wi-Fi was, but he knew the phone was working because of it.

The whole experience for Darnell was surreal. It was like they just threw him out. No help, no guidance on where to go but a piece of paper, and he was expected to figure the rest out. For the past 25 years, he had been confined to their walls, being told what to do, when to eat, how to move, and under their surveillance, but the minute he was released, they wanted nothing to do with him. It was like they threw him on the side of the road and told him to figure it out. While it was an adjustment for him and challenging to find his own way, he was just happy to be free and go home.

He finally got a chance to call his mom and let her know what was going on so that he could get picked up when he got to Detroit. His mother said that she would be picking him up, and that was the plan until he called Asia, and she said she was coming to get him instead. When Darnell finally got to Detroit, he had seen Asia before she had seen him. She noticed him, and he started walking to her. Once they got to each other, they gave each other the biggest hug, and of course, Asia started to cry. This was what they had been waiting for for so long, and it was finally happening. The moment and feeling was indescribable.

The first stop was Darnell's mother's house. Walking into her house after so many years felt like a rush to him. Everything they had gone through growing up and the memories that were made all came back to them by walking into that house. Darnell and Mann's room had been turned into a guest room. Derrick's room still looked like it was his. Walking into it just brought back that day, his mother told him about how she found him and tried to throw it back into the back of his mind.

Those first few days back home, Darnell just took it all in. He was happy and overwhelmed at the same time. It was an indescribable feeling for him. The more people found out he was home, the more phone calls came to the house from people wanting to talk to him, see how he was doing, and even send him money.

All Darnell could think about was what some of his first moves were going to be now that he was home. One thing he knew was that he needed to get a job and his State ID. Darnell's Uncle Ivan was a lawyer, and he was married to Darnell's Aunt Mel. Ivan went a step further and offered to get his driver's license cleared, being that Darnell's license had been suspended since 1987. He pulled some strings, filed the clearance papers, and got everything cleared up so that Darnell didn't have any fees to pay and get his license with no issues.

What seemed so simple ended up being a frustrating process for Darnell. When Darnell was released he was given an ID card and was told he could use it as a temporary solution until he got his official state ID. Darnell took his temporary ID card, birth certificate, and social security card to the Secretary of State's office so that he could get started on getting his license. However, when he got there, they told him that in order to get his license, he needed at least 5 forms of ID, and the ID that was given to him by the prison was not one of them.

As he was looking at the list of what he needed, he recalled the prison forwarding his mail to his mother's house, and some of the paperwork his uncle filed also had his name and mother's address, which gave him two more forms of ID. When he went back to the secretary's office, they told him he would need an educational transcript. Darnell hadn't been in school since 1987, and he never graduated; how did they expect him to get his transcripts after so much time. He called his Aunt Chrissy, and she told him what to do and where to go. Darnell thought that was just another hurdle, and it only took 5 minutes to get done. He went back again and was able to register for his written test. Later on, he took his road test and finally got his license.

Going through that process was another confirmation for Darnell that the system is set up for you to fail. It was so frustrating trying to get his license, and for someone like him, he knew an easier way to do it. Had he still had his connection to the streets or even attempted to reconnect with them, he could have paid somebody to get him a fake ID and kept pushing. However, Darnell didn't want to go down that road again. He wanted something different this time around and took the frustration on the chin. Think about the ones who don't think the way Darnell did? So many of them fold under pressure because it is easier.

As Darnell was still adjusting, it was time for his first walk-through from his supervised release officer. Darnell had already had the conversation with his mother about what could not be in the house, being that she and her boyfriend both had permits to carry and registered guns in the house. He let her know that he could not be around them, and they were removed. During the officer's walk-through, she came across an ammo box and a million thoughts ran through Darnell's head because he knew that the box could be considered a violation. He started recalling a couple of situations where he knew of someone getting a year in prison for every bullet that was found. Luckily for him, she knew that he was not aware that the box was there and told him she would end the walk through and come back the next day. She spoke with his mother and expressed the severity of everything being out of the house when she came back to do her walk-through. Darnell and his mother spent the rest of that day shaking the house down to make sure there was nothing in there that could put him in a bad spot. The next day, when she came again to do the walk through, everything was good, and his living arrangements were cleared.

After she cleared him officially, Darnell expected that his release office would be assisting him in finding a job or getting enrolled in school. She did none of the sort. Darnell went out on his own, and not only did he get a job, but he also ended up with two. When he let his release officer know about his progress, she seemed so surprised at what he had been able to do in just 3 weeks of being home.

For Darnell, life on the other side of the fence was hard, but it was also whatever you made it to be and he knew what he wanted to do so he wasn't going to let anything make him fold. It wasn't that he didn't think he could do it, he just needed to figure out how. There was so much that he still didn't know, such as how to use a phone, how to use a computer, or even what type of clothes to wear. It was a wrap around adjustment for him. What he did know was that he wanted to make a difference this time around. He was thinking differently, feeling differently, and seeing things in a different light.

Although Darnell was thinking differently, it was an adjustment in him recognizing his freedom. At times, it felt like he didn't know what to do with so much freedom. While in prison, Darnell felt like he was mentally free and physically locked up and when he thought of coming home, he thought he would be free in both aspects. However, now that he was home, he felt like he was mentally locked up but physically free. It was hard not to get wrapped up in his prison ways, and it was a battle for him. While he was in prison, one of his rules was to never get into it with his cellmate because when the doors closed, he never wanted to sleep with one eye open. Coming home and living with his mother, mentally, it was like having another cellmate. He wanted to stay out of her way and not cause any problems because he couldn't get into it with his cellmate. This was a hard adjustment for him because the way he looked at it was that he was 49 years old and back living with his mother. He had been on his own for so long. It was an adjustment for his mother as well because she had been used to living alone for quite some time herself. At times, Darnell would startle her when moving around the house, and he hated the thought of feeling like his mother was scared of him. Moving in with his mother was like he was moving in with a different cellmate who had already been there for years. They already have a routine and do things a certain way. They were used to their normal lives, and he had to try to find a way to fit into that. In prison, routines and normalcy were what helped the day go by. Knowing that, Darnell didn't want to disrupt his mother's normal. It felt like walking on eggshells, and it was hard on both of them.

Trying to adjust to his new relationship with his mother was challenging, but it was also a challenge in his new relationship with his children. Even though Darnell never went too long without talking to or seeing his kids, it was as if they had to learn who each other was on this side of the fence, and it wasn't easy. He knew them behind those walls, but he didn't know them without them. He had to get to know them and their ways on a larger scale. These weren't monitored visits and timed phone calls. He was a short-term dad in prison trying to adjust to being a long-term dad with grown kids that he didn't know. He had to make time for him to get to know them and for them to get to know him.

Darnell started to feel like he had a better relationship with everyone when he was in prison. You would have thought they would have gotten better when he came home, but that wasn't the case at the start. His relationship with his mother was not good. The relationships with his brother and sister weren't good, and no one was truly working on it. The relationships with his kids weren't good. There was no understanding of each other on all sides, and it was hard on everybody. It put Darnell back in a mental prison because while he was actually in prison, none of this was happening. He wanted their old relationships back, but he didn't want to be back in prison for it. Being that his mind kept going back to being in prison, it kept him there anyway.

Not only was Darnell trying to get to know everybody all over again, but he was trying to get to know himself too. He didn't even know his own identity anyway. He was a stranger in his own body while trying to relearn the way society worked. Even though there was so much to learn and adapt to. Darnell never looked at it as him missing out on so much. He looked at his situation as a challenge that he was ready to accept to secure a different future for him. He embraced learning and finding his way. It was constant for him. He knew that if he didn't continue to educate himself, he would get left behind, and that wasn't an option for him. He got a second chance at doing life his way, and he wasn't going to waste it being worried about what he couldn't change.

Chapter 24

THE REBUILD

D arnell started recalling the things he said he would do when he was sentenced. He told himself and the judge that if he was to ever come home, wherever he was he would start his own business and build up the community. Those thoughts started creeping back up on him, reminding him of what he was supposed to be doing. Darnell had written down all his plans and goals and his girlfriend Adriann had told him about him making a vision board. Darnell's mother had a clipboard laying around and he took the clipboard , put all his plans and goals on it and then hung it up in his room as his vision board. Darnell's motivation rose even more.

At this time Darnell had gotten into fitness training at the gym he was working at. While working there, he started paying attention to how they did things. Darnell was getting paid $12 per hour, and they were charging members $35-$45 per training session, and they were only 20 minutes. Darnell was expected to train and advertise as a sales associate for the gym whenever he was not in a training session. However, once he did the math on how much he was getting paid compared to how much they were making off of his fitness training, he said he could do it on his own and decided to do just that. Darnell started looking into ways for him to start his own fitness training business. In the midst of him starting this new journey, Covid-19 came in and shut the world down. During Covid, air travel, non-essential stores, hotels, gyms and more had closed their doors. Having no access to any gyms put a pause on his plans. A few months after being shut down, states started to open back up slowly. Darnell had found out that Ohio had opened before Detroit with more lenient Covid protocols and figured going to Ohio would be better for him. He started going back and forth from Detroit to Youngstown, checking out different gyms and how they were being run. He came across a gym that really sparked his attention and talked to the owner, Doug. Darnell was so interested in how Doug ran his gym because it was designed for personal trainers. The gym was kind of structured like a barbershop, you build up your client and pay monthly booth rent. One of Darnell's first ideas was to host a kickbox fitness class. Doug loved Darnell's idea because it wasn't something he had going on at his gym, and now Darnell was offering it. This was exactly what Darnell was looking for. It was all he needed to get his foot in the door to birth his business, which he named "Determined Life." Sound familiar? He was doing it again. He checked the scenery, asked questions, and planned to plant himself in Youngstown. But this time around, his move to Youngstown was for all the right reasons.

Darnell had started getting closer to Adriann's daughter, Shalise. Everyone called her Boogie. They started building a bond over the interest they both shared in real estate. They had been looking so much into it together that they decided to become business partners. Their newfound partnership brought Darnell's second business venture, DAB Property Group, to life. DAB stood for "Darnell, Adriann and Boogie".

So far looking back at his vision board, Darnell realized he was bringing his goals to life. Mostly, everything he had written on his board was happening. The only goal that didn't seem to have motion behind it from his board was his start to rebuilding the community. However, that all changed when Darnell and Shimmie reconnected. Shimmie had been in prison for 26 years after being wrongfully convicted of murder. He had gotten out a few months after Darnell. Their reconnection did not start instantly. They had spoken on the phone a few times, but that's all it was. They had both seemed pretty distant and kind of tried to feel each other out. It wasn't until Shimmie threw a birthday party that Darnell attended that they actually got to really talk more in depth that night. One thing Darnell was big on upon coming home was not being around people who were still trapped in the streets. He didn't want any part of it. Darnell didn't put his guard down with Shimmie until he was sure that Shimmie was in the same place as him with being done with the streets. After talking with him that night, they both realized that they were on the same page and even had a couple similar goals they were going after. Shimmie let Darnell know about his R.E.S.P.E.C.T organization. R.E.S.P.E.C.T is a non profit organization which stands for (Reaching Everyday Solutions Positively and Encouraging Community Togetherness.) Shimmie's R.E.S.P.E.C.T program focuses on community development and youth mentorship. This was the type of work Darnell wanted to get into. This was what he meant when he said he wanted to rebuild the community. Darnell decided to get involved in the R.E.S.P.E.C.T program and learn as much as he could. He had some ideas of his own but he never sat down and mapped out exactly what it was going to take. However, Shimmie started his mentorship program while he was in prison and when he came home he connected with the United Returning Citizens and was able to continue implementing his program for the community.

One of the first projects was a non-violent rally put together by Shimmie on the South Side of Youngstown. Darnell was a volunteer for the event. The message of the rally was that they wanted to rebuild the same community they helped destroy. The rally started on the corner of Hillman and Warren where they made their first drug sale, and made its way down the hill ending at the Oak Hill Collaborative where they arranged multiple speakers to talk to the community about what could be done to save the lives of the youth. That rally made it even more real for Darnell. He knew this was what he wanted to be doing and could see it all beginning to come together. It helped him to get a better idea of how he wanted to be involved because although he knew he wanted to help the community, he didn't know how he would go about it. This was the spark to point him in the right direction.

While Darnell was focusing on the door opening to speak with the youth, another door of opportunity was opened up for him as well. At this time, Darnell had been home for 9 months. It was December 19, 2019 and Darnell made a Facebook post reminiscing about the day he was granted Clemency.

"At this time 3 years ago, I was sitting in a prison cell with a Life Sentence. Not knowing what was about to happen, but I knew I was losing hope of ever getting out. Knowing that President Obama had

a month left in office. Fearing that I would spend the rest of my life in prison. Hoping that I would get a call from my lawyer saying that I was going home or just that my Life Sentence had been commuted to anything! Time was not on my side, then I heard keys. Two CO's was walking by and one of them stopped, said, oh Walker, the counselor wants you to come to his office at 2:30 pm. I said okay thank you. Soon as he continued to walk by, I put a blanket up over my bars. (Old prison), anyway, I then started to have a panic attack, which I never ever had before, so I told myself to get it together. I had seen a few people I knew get this same call. So I knew what it was; waiting those 3 hours was the longest time of my life. When I finally made it to the office and got the call from Allison Terrell and Linda DelaCourt-Summers. Hearing them say, Congratulations Darnell, your Life Sentence has been commuted to 360 months. I was too excited to cry and too anxious to call my family and tell them. Now 3 years later, I am blessed to be able to post my thoughts of what happened then. Thank you President Obama and thank you Ali and Linda! These 2 beautiful women fought real hard for me when they did not have to. I learned during this process that these are the kind of people they are. So thank you again, President Obama, for granting me clemency and being fortunate enough to have these 2 amazing people cross my path."

A long-time friend of his, named Melissa Brown reached out to him after seeing his post. She worked at a behavior rehabilitation center and asked Darnell to come and speak to her group. He said yes and had officially been booked for his first speaking engagement.

Melissa had no idea that it was Darnell's first time speaking. Darnell had a conversation with the chaplain and told him he had never spoken before, and that is how she found out. She had assumed from his FB post that this was a part of what he had already been doing. However, Darnell wasn't really a talkative person, and he had never done anything like this before, so he didn't know what to expect but was up for the challenge. The group sat around in a circle and that made things a lot more comfortable for him. After telling his story and speaking positive messages over the group another spark happened and here Darnell was again finding out more about what his community work will look like. This led to Darnell being asked to speak again at the Trumbull Correctional Institution by Sausirae, who knew of Darnell and worked at the prison. He was asked to speak twice that day, once in the morning and again in the afternoon. This time, it was a little different than speaking to a group in a circle. He was speaking at a podium. During the first session, as he's reading through the speech he had written, it starts to get really hot, and Darnell sweats through his clothes. Alina, Adriann's sister who also worked at the prison, notices and brings him some paper towels. Darnell didn't know what was going on; he had done such a great job the first time, but his nerves were getting the better of him. After the session was over, they took a break for lunch. During the break, a couple of COs came to talk to Darnell about his obvious nerves. Alina explains, "Darnell, you just came from a place like that. If anybody understands what you went through, it's these inmates. You can connect to them in a way that we can't, and you have a story; the only one that can tell that story is you." Darnell took in everything she said. She was right. He begins asking himself why he even got so nervous all of a sudden and gets ready for the second session to speak again. Darnell did the unthinkable. Not only did he tell his story in a way that hit home for the inmates, he spoke for 2 hours and 45 minutes straight! The man of "not too many" words had a mouthful to say that day. When he went out there to speak again, he felt that it was his purpose and called to speak in that room so he gave it his all. He knew he didn't want anybody else to go through what he went through, and if his words could draw even one person away from the streets, that's what he wanted to be doing. This led to Darnell being invited back a 2nd and 3rd time and even Shimmie speaking with him. They were so impressed with them that they proposed to have them come more times throughout the year.

Shortly after soaking this breakthrough in, Shimmie had gotten a speaking engagement set up at Chaney High School to speak to their boys, and Darnell was a part of that booking as well. Then came East High School and even another at Chaney Middle School. The door to the youth had officially been opened, and Darnell's purpose was even bigger.

While Darnell's vision board was coming to life, things he had never even thought about started to come into play as well. For someone who was never a big talker, he seemed to always come across opportunities to use his voice. A collaboration between Shimmie, Darnell, Bryant Youngblood, and Kelan Bilal brought together a podcast called "Pros & Cons". Darnell and Shimmie were considered to be the cons and Bryant and Kelan were considered to be the pros. The concept was to get the different points of view from both sides. Darnell and Shimmie's struggles led them to sell drugs and Kelan and Bryant's struggles led them to education. They hosted several guests and discussed various topics that helped to empower both sides of the fence. Shimmie put together another podcast called "Beefin 'to Brotherhood" and brought a group of men together, including Darnell, to discuss how they went from beefing in the 90s to working together in the community and building a brotherhood with one another. There were 9 men who participated in the first podcast episode, and of those men, Darnell could only recall not having beef with 2. He remembers days when some of them couldn't see each other without an argument or sometimes even a shootout and now they were sitting across from each other talking about the work they were doing in the community and how to reach the youth who are having the same beefing struggles they had back then. These podcasts were powerful and Darnell was using his voice and his story in ways he had never even thought about.

It started dawning on Darnell that moving back to Youngstown again was the right decision. He was exactly where he was supposed to be. The purpose of his moving to Youngstown the first time was for him to sell drugs. It was the blueprint he thought he needed to get his Hollywood star. Now, his purpose of being in Youngstown is to rebuild what he broke and create a different kind of legacy. His new purpose got him another shot at a different Hollywood moment and it hit differently for him. One of his fitness clients was a hair stylist and she had been talking about Darnell to one of her clients. Her name was Madonna Chism Pickard, and she hosted a morning show called Community Connection on the 21 WFMJ news. After hearing so many great things about Darnell and his story, she reached out to him to ask for an interview. This was big for Darnell. All he could think about was the only many times his name and face had been on the news, and it was never for anything positive, but now that was about to change. Madonna made sure Darnell was comfortable with the questions she asked and was even better at pulling things out of him that he didn't even know were there. The interview went so well that she invited him to come again the following week and this time, people had questions for him. Someone had even asked Darnell what they needed to do to try and get clemency for their son. Darnell was constantly finding a purpose for his story, and it always made things more clear for him.

Darnell has a whole new way of thinking now. He used to think about his life sentence and say, "Why me?". He always felt like the world was against him because of the cards he was dealt. Now, Darnell believes everything happens for a reason and it will always give you a better understanding. It's on you to recognize the problem, understand how to learn from the problem and then know how to grow from it. When you realize that, you'll have a better understanding of life and a real shot at true freedom. Did Darnell pay a high price for his freedom? Definitely. However, At this time, Darnell has been home for 4 years now and the things he's learned and experienced in this short amount of time has been priceless to him. He's embracing the challenges along the way and learning what he can through his journey. He knows you have to be willing to grow through it to get through it and you should never give up along the way. While you're on the journey recognize the right people to have around you and don't let anyone interfere with where you are going.

If Darnell could go back and talk to his 19 year old self he would tell him, "Work smarter, not harder." If only he knew then what he knows now. 19 year old Darnell only knew one way to make real money, but there was so much more than that one lane. He had one way and one drug. That was his only plan. He didn't know that in order to truly have financial freedom, he needed multiple lanes. His streams of money started and stopped at the streets, and it's not just about the money either. It's about what the money came with. All money doesn't come with looking over your shoulder all the time. It doesn't come with shootouts and running from the cops. You don't have to worry about who to trust. Darnell wishes he could have told himself to find the right people to be around. The ones who help build you up and get you where you want to be the right way. There is power in building connections and being in the right circles. If only he knew that his way then wasn't the only way for him. If he could have that conversation with his 19 year old self, he would be rich by now. Not rich in terms of just money, but rich in knowledge and opportunity. Even though Darnell can't go back in time to change the choices he made, that doesn't mean he can't make different choices today.

Darnell spent years fighting for his freedom from the streets. His addiction to them made it hard for him to get out. Even though he was tired of what the streets came with, he couldn't find his way out. His only way out was through, and it took being sentenced to life in prison to finally be free from it all. That was the price. His freedom almost cost him his life, but today, he stands here as a free man, determined to rebuild everything he broke, and his story is still being written.

Made in the USA
Columbia, SC
10 July 2024

38432709R00065